"*Life*
is short and
so is
money"

Bertolt Brecht
The Threepenny Opera

Books to make
your life go further
at Waterstone's

MONEY

49

Editor: Bill Buford
Deputy Editor: Ursula Doyle
Managing Editor: Claire Wrathall
Editorial Assistant and Picture Researcher: Cressida Leyshon
Contributing Editor: Robert McSweeney

Managing Director: Catherine Eccles
Financial Controller: Geoffrey Gordon
Marketing and Advertising: Sally Lewis
Circulation Manager: Lesley Palmer
Subscriptions: Kelly Cornwall
Publishing Assistant: Nichola Bath

Picture Editor: Alice Rose George
Executive Editor: Pete de Bolla
US Publisher: Anne Kinard, Granta, 250 West 57th Street, Suite 1316, New York, NY 10107.

Editorial and Subscription Correspondence: Granta, 2–3 Hanover Yard, Noel Road, London N1 8BE. Telephone: (071) 704 9776.
Fax: (071) 704 0474. Subscriptions: (071) 704 0470.
A one-year subscription (four issues) is £21.95 in Britain, £29.95 for the rest of Europe and £36.95 for the rest of the world.

Cover by Senate. Back cover photograph: Popperfoto

Granta 49, Winter 1994
ISBN 0-14-014088-3

'*The Informers* shows the work of a writer at the peak of his powers... The book takes us from the first to the seventh circles of hell, from Salinger to De Sade, and in doing so shows that *American Psycho* was no gratuitous exercise, but a keynote text in the development of a major writer's oeuvre' **WILL SELF**

PICADOR

HISTORY: THE HOME MOVIE

Craig Raine

A twentieth century landscape...
written to be read out loud

Unabridged and read by the author on 4 cassettes   £12.50

Also available in paperback

CONTENTS

1st January - 31st December 1995

Abertawe
Swansea

" *The writer is both
communicator and comforter.
Our year will be an
imaginative appraisal and
approval of these writers and
thinkers, be they philosophers,
songwriters, poets or
journalists.*"

Swansea's UK Year of Literature and writing 1995 will be a celebration with the world of the rich culture of Wales, its two languages and literatures past and present. As we approach the new Millennium it is equally appropriate that "the largest and most ambitious literature festival ever" should cast its net wide by welcoming the finest poets, songwriters, dramatists, screenwriters, novelists and journalists of our time.

Writers participating include:
Michele Roberts, Elvis Costello, James Kelman, Sara Dunant and Jack Mapanje.

For further information & to join our FREE mailing list for the year, please complete and return to: UK Year of Literature & Writing 1995, Somerset Place, Swansea SA1 1SE.

PLEASE PRINT CLEARLY

Name ....

Address ....

.... Post Code ....

UK YEAR OF LITERATURE AND WRITING 1995
BLWYDDYN LLENYDDIAETH A LLENYDDA Y D.G 1995

GRANTA

RICHARD RAYNER
RICH RICH RICH

My life began at Cambridge, the moment I walked through the Emmanuel College gate and stood on the smooth, uneven stones within the cloisters. I loved the bad sherry and the rotten dinners, which I ate, gowned, in Emmanuel Hall. I was happy, spending too much on a bike that was stolen at once, so that I then had to spend too much on another; I adored my philosophy lecturers: Bernard Williams, boyish and brilliant, apologizing because he was having an off day; Casimir Lewy, who'd known Wittgenstein, wheezing and cackling: 'Of course two and two is four, it's quite clear, quite obvious, unless of course you are an . . . *Ogggsford* logician.' I loved Cambridge by day in the rain, a sandstone Garden of Eden, dripping and dank, and at night, when the fog rolled knee-high off the river and the baby spruce trees around the duck pond looked like cowled monks. I loved that at Cambridge I could be anyone I wanted to be.

This was 1974. And in between the students of King's College, who still wore kaftans, took drugs and toted copies of Marx and Marcuse, and the squirely types in tweed jackets at Magdalene (some of whom, only five years later, would be young MPs in Margaret Thatcher's first government), it was easy to fit in. Anything was possible.

I had an academic tutor, a personal tutor and a moral tutor, the latter a tall man with big ears and a drooping, horse-like face. Though a Christian, he'd written a controversial book, the crux of which was his argument that Christ wasn't literally the Son of God. Christ was only a metaphor. When I told him that I was having trouble with ethics, there was a forced, awkward moment. 'In the intellectual rather than the practical sense I trust,' he said, and exploded with a nervous gale of laughter.

In fact the trouble I was having with ethics was that I'd never thought about them before—in any sense. I had opinions on almost every subject, could argue any position and believed in almost nothing. I grew up, not necessarily with the belief, but with the feeling powerfully impressed on me, that life was a question of surviving, of making it through, not getting caught. I wasn't interested in politics. When people told me that England was, and always had been, in the throes of a class war to the death, I listened with a smile. I wasn't waiting for a revolution. I was waiting for romantic love. My ideas of art and beauty came from Blake, Byron and Emily Brontë, not to mention the gorgeous third movement of Mahler's Sixth Symphony, a recording of which I'd stolen from the public library. I was waiting for happiness, and at Cambridge I was happier than I'd ever been.

I can't remember when I first met Pete, a self-consciously cool figure in boots, jeans and a black velvet jacket. A Wykehamist, he smoked Marlboro, had met Harold Pinter and contrived to carry himself like a debonair Latin-American revolutionary. He had a moustache, a selection of silk scarves, a beret. His eyes always narrowed a little as he cupped his hand to light up the next fag. His parents, I eventually learned, had a flat in Mayfair, an estate in Norfolk. There was talk of 'the house in Chelsea', which had been bought for the kids. Peter Sellers lived next door. Yet he wore all this easily: Pete's wealth was only conspicuous when boxloads of salt 'n' vinegar crisps were delivered to his rooms. We ate packets by the gross. His father, a refugee who'd fled Czechoslovakia penniless in 1937, now ran, among much else, the company that owned the company that made Golden Wonder crisps.

At the end of the Christmas term, I went with Pete to Chelsea. The family house, the one next door to Peter Sellers, was squashed and narrow, but seemed to go up forever: five, six floors. The rooms were like little boxes, all different shapes and sizes—some with angled ceilings, others with curving white plaster walls. There was a girl in the room next to mine. I met her when I went upstairs to unpack, and a face popped around the door. 'Oh, so you're here,' she said. Red hair, pale skin—that was as much as I had the chance to take in. There was a shout from below.

'Rich!'

Pete had decided to buy a suit. His sisters—and the other women in the house, of whom there seemed to be many—heaped scorn. The suit was very expensive; he had no cash; besides, the shop would have closed by the time we got there.

The redhead glanced at me from the end of the room, next to the record-player. She seemed to want me to join her, or so I hoped, but then Pete, who had been on the phone, fingered his Zapata moustache and said, 'Come on. We're off.'

Ten minutes later we were sashaying through swing doors into the Ritz. The carpet was thick and springy, taking into itself all the noise of London, leaving a pleasant murmur and babble. A soft, golden light came from chandeliers high above. People glided by, dressed in tuxedos and evening gowns, pulling on white silk scarves and coats, ready for dinner, the theatre, the night ahead. A uniformed concierge came bustling towards us; we were, I assumed, about to be thrown out.

'*Mister Peter*,' he said in a soft voice, delighted. 'How nice to see you again, Sir.' He handed Pete a white envelope stuffed with ten pound notes. 'Please do come and see us again, Sir, and give my best to Sir Joseph and Lady Joseph.'

'My parents used to keep a suite there,' Pete said as we hailed another cab and rushed back to the King's Road. He had asked the shop to stay open, carrying all this off as though it were nothing special. The suit was of a gorgeous, deep bottle-green velvet—price 250 guineas.

I wasn't envious. I was dazzled.

The next evening there was a dinner party in the living-room, so tiny and neat it resembled a doll's house. Beforehand, women darted about in various states of undress. I wasn't sure which were Pete's sisters; he eyed them all with the same cool disdain.

I was seated next to the redhead from upstairs. Her eyes were bloodshot as if she'd been crying. She talked to me about her boyfriend, an Italian actor named Franco. Her father disapproved. He himself was a writer-turned-film-star, a famous talent, tyrant and nutcase. He didn't want her involved in show business or anyone connected with it.

'We just had the most bloody awful row,' she said. 'Daddy's such a stinker.' She sighed. 'What about yours?'

'He's dead.'

She looked at me as if noticing me for the first time. She touched my sleeve with her hand. 'I'm so sorry,' she said.

'Happened a long time ago. Cancer,' I said. We got on well from then on, and she was even impressed when I recited a couple of poems by Blake, a new tactic.

Afterwards, hunting for more wine in the kitchen, Pete asked, 'What's this about your father being dead?'

My heart gave a bump. I had to think for a moment. I'd told him something else, that my father was up in Yorkshire, a novelist turned publishing executive. I'd told him, in effect, that my *stepfather* was my father.

'Oh, it was such a long time ago,' I said. 'He died just after I was born. I've always thought of my stepfather as if he were my father.'

Pete shrugged. 'It's good that you get on with him so well.'

I leaned against the door for a moment before returning to the table. I was rubbery with fear and relief—as if someone had burst into my soul with a camera.

My real father hadn't died from cancer. He wasn't dead at all, though for many years I wished he were. He'd been born in 1921 and had grown up in Bradford when it was still booming. He was christened John Bertram Rayner but was always called Jack—Flash Jack, Black Jack, Jack the Lad. At sixteen his first job was in the Victorian heart of the city at a wool merchant's—sweet with the smell of lanolin, recording what came and went from the warehouse: not only wool, but camel-hair from Egypt, mink and buffalo skins from America, a crate from Shanghai with thousands of pigtails inside. In the late 1930s he met my mother—'a little stick of dynamite in grey overalls,' he remembered—but during the war, when he served in the RAF, they didn't see much of each other, and afterwards, soon after the birth of my sister, my mother realized it was all wrong. She picked up the phone, and a stranger's voice asked if she'd heard about the other woman he was keeping in a town just a couple of miles away; he'd rented a flat and was giving the woman twenty-five pounds a week. No wonder money was always tight.

I was born eight years later, the result of a reconciliation in the back of a Rover motor car outside Otley. My father assured me it was more romantic than it sounds. He wasn't like other fathers, I soon realized. He loved cricket and worked the way people seemed to work in the movies—not a lot. He had a thin moustache, an air of suave indifference borrowed from Fred Astaire and was interested in any woman who wasn't my mother. He was often away from home, and during these unexplained

absences the police would come to our house, asking if we knew where he was. I must have been three or four when he told my mother that he was going out for a pint of milk. He came back two weeks later with a bottle in each hand, saying, 'I got two, just to be on the safe side.' Another early memory: I was with him in a Mini Cooper S, a small and very fast car of the 1960s. My father had competed in the Monte Carlo Rally and was a skilled driver; he never did get along with speed limits. On this occasion he

Above: Jack Rayner on his twenty-first birthday in 1942.

15

grinned, nodding in the direction of the speedometer, which said 105 mph, and took his hands from the wheel. He sang, 'Yes, we have no bananas, we have no bananas today.'

It was during the hard winter of 1962–3 that my mother walked out at last. She never came back, and he never got over it. He left Bradford, and I went with him to live in the North Wales seaside resort of Llandudno, where he owned a garage and various other small businesses, including a coffee bar he called 'Boz' after Dickens's early pen-name. His favourite characters were Bill Sikes and, of course, Mr Micawber.

I was nine. My father had found a boarding-school nearby. The school, a Victorian building with turrets and battlements recently painted white, was approached up a hill. Staff members were old and eccentric—monsters, even. The lavatories had no doors. The dormitories had no heating. The classrooms had radiators which, even though scalding, were never warm enough to melt the ice that formed on the windows. Offences were punished by beatings with a split cane in Room 100. But my greatest dread was Sunday mornings, when we were required to write a letter to our parents. There was no point in writing to my father, since I saw him every week, so I wrote to my mother; and there was one particular master—bald, eyes full of anger—who, when all the letters had been collected, regularly called me to the front of the class and asked . . . 'Mrs M. Michie?' Didn't I have parents of my own to write to? I whispered that Mrs Michie was my mother, that she'd married again, but he always interrupted: 'This boy doesn't even *know his own name.*' And then he invited the other boys to laugh; they duly obliged.

I started to suffer from migraines, stroboscopic shimmerings at the edge of my vision. I had a dreamy sensation that the world was being snipped away—followed by two hours of a blinding headache, then vomiting until I had only bile left to retch. The attacks became so frequent that I was allowed to sit them out in a darkened room.

Meanwhile, my father's businesses were going badly. He had debts and was in trouble with the police. People were after him, he said, and not just in Llandudno; they were on their way down

from Bradford as well. He cried about my mother. I hated him for being drunk, not understanding how desperate he was. One night I went into his bedroom and found a mountain of banknotes on a table. They were so crisp and new that they creaked gently in the draught from the door. Soon after, his clothes were found in a pile on the beach: my father was missing, presumed drowned.

2

During my second Cambridge year I panicked. I'd found my great romantic love, in the shape of Janie, a student at the local teacher-training college, and I thought, for the first time, of my life and what I was going to do with it. I suddenly felt that a career was in order and that a bad degree in philosophy wasn't going to help. I decided that my calling would be the law—ironic given that I was my father's son, but the irony passed me by, as irony usually did,

Above: Richard Rayner.

and I took a vacation job with a big West End firm of solicitors. I shuttled between meetings, sped in taxis to retrieve folders from mouldering town hall basements, and was fired when I was discovered using the firm's headed notepaper for job applications to other companies just in case my legal calling didn't work out. Undeterred I began my third year as a law student, determined to make up for all the time I'd frittered away. I pored over the *All England Law Reports*, silently mouthing cases from tort and criminal law, and asked Janie to marry me because it all seemed part of the procedure. She was angry because I hadn't thought the idea through, and then she was angry because I wasn't upset that she refused me. So I rediscovered books.

The occasion was a friend's visit to my rooms. He looked around, astonished. 'You don't have any books,' he said. 'How very bizarre. You must be the only person in Cambridge without his shelves stuffed.'

It was as if he'd announced, 'You don't exist.' Books had always been important to me: how could this have happened?

I went to Heffers, the big university bookshop, and signed up for an account. I bought Dryden's *Poems*, a thick, red paperback, as well as Nabokov's *The Defence* and *The Clown* by Heinrich Böll. Heffers was like a network of caves, one book-filled room leading to another, inviting and snug. The smells of ink and paper, the very shelves themselves, were a reassuring arm around the shoulder. The future would be fine. In there, I was no longer flashing about, but earthed, grounded. I went to Heffers every day, two or three times a day, and then to Cambridge's other bookshops. I haunted those places. I couldn't control myself. It was suddenly necessary to possess all sorts of books. The new collection of poems by Robert Lowell. Who could live without *Gray's Anatomy*? Others might have been able to resist Boswell's *London Journal*, but not me. Hugh Thomas's *Spanish Civil War* would more than do, as well as anything by Raymond Chandler. The fever soon touched every genre.

I thought I'd steal a book, just one, to see if I had the nerve. I began with *The Sermons of John Donne*, the Cambridge University Press edition, quite plain, with a tan-and-red dust-jacket and handsome black boards. The paper inside was thick and stiffish, with the sweet, yellow colour of Cornish ice-cream. Reading the sermon given at St Paul's on Christmas Day, 1621, I tasted bliss:

> If thou canst take this light of reason that is in thee, this poor snuffe that is almost out in thee, thy faint of dimme knowledge of God, that riseth out of the light of nature, if thou canst in those embers, those cold ashes, find out one small coale, and wilt take the pain to kneell downe, and blow that coale with thy devout *Prayers*, and light thee a little candle . . .

I thought I'd found my salvation, my 'one small coale', and for a week I carried the *Sermons* with me everywhere, the only time I've had a glimmer of what it might be to have faith. I didn't dare tell anyone, and when the feeling went out again I was both disappointed and a little relieved because I wasn't sure I knew how to keep the flame burning.

I had in fact stolen my first book when I was fourteen—a paperback edition of *Dracula*; the second was Nik Cohn's *Awopbopaloobopalapbamboom*, the Paladin edition, a lovely thing with a Guy Peellart illustration of Elvis on the jacket. But now I couldn't be stopped. I stole a first edition of *Scoop*—Waugh had done the jacket art himself—priced at seventy-five pounds by the Heffers second-hand and antiquarian department. I stole the sturdy and solemn-looking Yale edition of the works of Samuel Johnson, one volume at a time. I walked away with Heinemann firsts of *Enderby Outside, Tremor of Intent* and *A Clockwork Orange. The Collected Poems of A. E. Housman*, Cape, 1939, buckram-bound. A cased, Cassell edition of *The Father Brown Stories*. Harold Nicolson's biography of George V; A. J .P. Taylor's *English History 1914–1945*; Ian McEwen's *First Love, Last Rites*; *Crash* by J. G. Ballard—those angular, oddly austere Cape jackets by Mon Mohan. I stole books every day. I went on expeditions first thing in the morning and again late in the afternoon, wearing a baggy jacket and marching out with books tucked in the armpit. The elegant John Murray edition of Byron's correspondence—I stole two at a time, Byron being slimmer than Johnson. I stole the war memoirs of David Lloyd George, brick-heavy, but I thought I'd better give them a whirl. The Neville

Spearman first of *A Walk on the Wild Side* by Nelson Algren was daftly underpriced at twenty-five pence on one of the stalls in the Market Square. I stole it anyway. I made the acquaintance of Saul Bellow, Norman Mailer, Philip Roth in the shape of various firsts stolen from all over town. I stole first editions of John Stuart Mill's autobiography, *Bleak House* by Dickens and *Ariel* by Sylvia Plath. *Black Mischief*, an old Chapman & Hall first, no dust-jacket, but handsome with mottled brown boards. A 1788 three-volume reprint of Johnson's *Rambler* essays, leather-bound, black, with gilt lettering. I loved those things. I stole Webster's *Collegiate Thesaurus*. *The First Raymond Chandler Omnibus* (Hamish Hamilton). *Finnegans Wake*. The Penguin P. G. Wodehouse novels, a rare excursion into paperback because I liked the artwork. Nabokov's *Ada*, *Lolita* and *The Gift*, as well as the four hardback volumes of his annotated translation of *Eugene Onegin*, boldly boosted in a Routledge boxed set from Bowes & Bowes.

I went mad. My head was a swarm of books. My rooms were full—books on the shelves, on the desk, piles of books on the chairs, books heaped against the skirting-boards.

'But, Rich, are you going to read all these?' asked Janie.

I was, I intended to, but that wasn't the point, I told her. They were lovely things, magical objects.

In Dee Brown's *Bury my Heart at Wounded Knee*, I read that in the months before the tribe's final defeat, a breakaway sect of Sioux Indians preached that the performance of a ritual known as the ghost dance would render them invulnerable. US Cavalry bullets would pass through and leave them unharmed. One evening, at about five-thirty, just as Heffers bookshop was about to close, with assistants already in position on either side of the glass door, I walked in and then carried out—openly, with no attempt at concealment—the buff-jacketed Harvard edition of W. Jackson Bate's biography of Keats and a white Chapman & Hall edition of Evelyn Waugh's *Sword of Honour* trilogy. As I walked out, I said under my breath, 'Won't see me, can't see me, won't see me, can't see me.'

One night, Janie came to my rooms and said we should spend some time apart. I sat down and wept. I played my last trump. I'd told her before that my father had died in a car crash when I was eight. Now I told her the truth about him: that he had vanished when I was a kid, having stolen the proceeds of fifty or so cars that he'd taken on credit from the British Motor Corporation and then sold; that he'd skedaddled with the cash (fifty thousand then; now, worth perhaps ten times as much), the *boodle* as he later called it, and had been on the run for eight years, abroad; that he'd reappeared the previous year at his mother's, my grandmother's, funeral, surrounded by police.

I was scared.

'He keeps sending me letters from jail,' I said. 'He's talking about coming to visit when he gets out.'

She reached for my hand. 'Oh, Rich.'

This revelation kept us together for another month.

3

In the Cambridge market square, there was an old brass fountain, tarnished with age and gummed up with drinking straws and cigarette butts and always smelling of urine. Drunks lolled on its steps, cradling tins of Carlsberg Special Brew or bottles of Anglia Sherry. The story was that one of them was a former don, an eccentric figure with his paunch and wild, grey hair and one of those plaid American hunting caps with the flaps at the sides. He was always shaking, as if shivering away some attack, or perhaps it was the DTs. Reputedly he'd been a brilliant philosophy lecturer, the protégé of Wittgenstein himself. Now, for the price of a pint, the master's one-time heir would recite the first five pages of *Tractatus-Logico-Philosophicus*.

I believed the story while finding it at the same time utterly unfeasible. I didn't see how anyone could snap so absolutely: at least I wouldn't. The world was there to be conquered, if you were any good. Failure could be handled, indeed *must* be handled; as Noël Coward had said, success was merely the infinite capacity for dealing with it. I was against moral slipping or any seepage of morale. I didn't believe in leaky boats.

I owed the college £652.75.

It doesn't seem such a huge sum now, nor did it a little while

21

later when my debts rose into the thousands, but at the time it might as well have been a million. One morning there was a letter in my pigeon-hole from the bursar. It was typed and said the college would stop me from graduating unless I paid up.

I burst out from within the cloisters, ran through Front Court, past the duck pond and up the four flights to my rooms.

Could they really stop me graduating? Did they have the power? I stuffed the letter into the back of a drawer and tried not to think about it. For the rest of the day I went about my business as usual: lectures, lunch, a game of cards with Pete afterwards. Six hundred and fifty-two pounds and seventy-five pence: otherwise I couldn't graduate. I considered going to the bursar's office, but the idea was too shaming. No, I had to get the money, which meant three options: borrow, earn or steal. My stepfather was the most likely candidate to borrow from, but I couldn't face him. That evening I wrote letters to three or four London papers asking for freelance work but I knew that this would take time, and that they might not get back to me at all. I didn't think of selling my books. Instead I picked up one to read, *In Hazard*, Richard Hughes's novel of a typhoon at sea. It was almost dark, but people were still playing on the tennis courts below.

I'm left-handed. As a child, I'd once been forced to write with my right hand: as a result, I can make my handwriting into pretty much what I want it to be. That evening, as a ball went *poing* against the rackets on the lawns outside my window, I practised my signature: first with my left hand, then my right. I had it sloping forwards, elegantly, then backwards, in a cramped, awkward style. I made it big and round; I made it a spidery scrawl; and, glancing up into the light of the standard lamp above my desk, I saw what I'd do.

I'd forge cheques.

The idea was so immediately exciting that I had to stand up, spin around the room a couple of times, then force myself to sit down. I was breathless. *I'd forge cheques.* I made a quick calculation of how many I'd have to do. Twenty-five. Twenty-five cheques and I'd be home clear. Simple.

I wasn't planning to become Al Capone. No one was going to get hurt. Fraud wasn't so bad; besides, this was a crime I knew

I could do. The procedure—writing out a cheque—was one I followed quite legally each time I went to the bank. And there was, in the ten thousand or so Cambridge students, an almost limitless supply of cheque-books, which weren't even used that often: cheque-books were kept in the students' rooms, which were usually unlocked. I could walk right in. It would be a breeze.

I'd have to go down to London—the activity would be conspicuous here: too few banks. Train fares would be an extra expense. Say thirty cheques. Say three cheques a day, once I got into the swing. Eleven or twelve days. A little over two weeks' work, that was all.

No, no, I thought, it's too silly.

I did nothing for a couple of days, but whether I was working, or having a drink in the bar, or playing cards with Pete, I was aware of the thought, not unpleasant—a thrilled pressure in the mind. A solution had presented itself. I had only to be bold.

Bank security worked slowly then. The system wasn't computerized. You could walk into any bank—it didn't have to be a branch of the one that had issued the cheques—write a cheque and hand over the guarantee card. It was up to the cashier to compare the signatures. The most cash you could get in one day in this manner was either thirty or fifty pounds, depending on how good a customer you were. Then the cheque went into the system.

I went to my own bank in the Market Square and studied the cashier after handing him my cheque. He barely glanced at the card before turning over the cheque and stamping it.

I put in some more thought. I'd have two clear days. The bank would take at least that long to distribute updated lists of stolen cards, even if the thefts were reported immediately. And then there was the question of where to start. I plumped for Churchill, one of the new colleges, a scattering of white concrete cubes at the western edge of town. I reasoned that distance would bring safety. Fewer people would recognize me. I thought no, it was too crazy; but then, somehow, the matter was settled in my mind—Churchill it would be.

Everything went so smoothly. It was the dinner hour, and the first room I tried was unlocked and empty. The cheque-book was in the centre drawer of the desk with the guarantee card

handily tucked between the stubs and the almost full portion of
the book that hadn't been used yet. At the back of the drawer, I
found a Visa card, an unexpected bonus.

My new life had begun.

I put on the blue suit, my only suit, and took the train to London,
where I went, first of all, not to a bank, but to Harrods, picking
out a white silk scarf and paying for it with the stolen Visa card. I
made my hand stiff and signed the name I'd been practising on the
way down: Sandy Wells. It was accepted without a glance, but, in
an excess of caution, I dawdled around the other counters,
holding my gift-wrapped package as though it were a bomb. Was
I being followed? Were store detectives on my trail? 'Oh, come
on,' I told myself. I couldn't believe it'd been so easy.

On the steps outside the Sloane Street entrance I made a
bargain, that if I counted to twenty and no one came after me, I
would never be caught—ever. Waiting and counting, with my eyes
shut, I heard the honking of taxis, the rumble and swish of the
revolving doors behind me. When I'd got to twenty, and no one
had come, I took out the scarf and draped it around my neck.

Then I was almost caught.

The bank was small, with only one cashier waiting behind
the security glass at the counter. The paint was yellow, a little
faded, and a poster on the wall said, COME TO FRANCE. I joined
the queue, thinking it was all to the good that there were so many
people, because the cashier would be pressed—in a hurry. A
clock told me it was nearly lunch-time—I had been in Harrods
for more than an hour without noticing. This was fun.

When at last I got to the front of the queue, I realized the
cheque-book wasn't in my hand but was still tucked away in the
briefcase. It would look awkward, fiddling around to get it out
now, I thought. No matter—I'd use Visa.

'I'd like to get some cash on my credit card,' I told the
cashier, a woman in her twenties. She wore a white blouse, and
the skin beneath her neck was freckled and pink, flushed from
the heat of the day. I looked into her eyes, and she looked back,
a little longer than I liked: it made me uncomfortable.

'Thirty pounds,' I said.

'This'll just take a minute,' she said and went to the back of the bank and picked up a phone. Had she guessed? I told myself not to be unreasonable. But then the woman in Harrods hadn't phoned anybody. I smiled at the chap behind me. I smiled at the fellow to my side and when I looked back at the counter I was still smiling. My smile was fixed like rigor mortis. All at once I realized that the routine of drawing money on a credit card was different from cashing a cheque or making a purchase, and involved phoning up Visa for clearance. Of course! And while there was no chance that a forged cheque would be spotted for a day or so, it was very possible that Visa already knew about the theft of this particular card. The knowledge was one phone call away. I wondered how the system worked. Were details of thefts fed into a computer which printed out lists? If so, how often? Daily? Hourly? Was the cashier on the phone to someone, a bespectacled Visa clerk going down a printout with a ruler, about to underline the name of Sandy Wells?

What was I doing? I was engaged in an activity that involved risk of capture, trouble, maybe jail, and I'd done not even the most basic research. I was sweating, I was faint. The yellow on the walls was brilliant and burning. The wrinkled French peasant clutching his baguette in the poster was leering at me. No one else seemed to have noticed. They couldn't know. Not possibly, not yet. The flushed cashier was still on the phone.

I picked up my briefcase and walked out. A middle-aged man in a suit gave me a look. There was a rumpus behind me when I reached the door. Someone called out, 'Sir,' but by then I was out into the midsummer heat of Knightsbridge. Without looking back, I scurried down the steps into the Underground, through the station, up the other side, across the street, down another entrance, then down the escalators and on to the platform as a northbound train rumbled in.

I didn't know how close I'd been to getting caught. It felt like very. But I still had the cheque-book and cheque-guarantee card. I would have to forget the disaster of the first bank and think instead of the success of Harrods, knowing that unless I made myself go into another bank immediately I'd never again have the nerve. When actors fluff their lines, the remedy is to get back on stage at once. The train stopped at Covent Garden, at Holborn: at Russell Square I got out, crossing the platform to catch a southbound train. Thirty seemed an awful lot of cheques now.

I'd learned a lesson. If anything felt wrong, for any reason, I must leave. I really didn't want to be caught.

On Bond Street, I went into the first bank I saw, joined a queue, wrote out a cheque, adding the signature only when at the counter. The cashier was another woman in her twenties. I looked her straight in the eye. I took care to pause, not for too long, counting the six fivers I'd asked for. I placed them inside my brown leather wallet with the word MEXICO embossed on the front, and only then, with a 'Thanks' and another smile at the cashier, did I leave.

With a little glow I walked down through Mayfair to a pub. For lunch I had a pint and a packet of Golden Wonder crisps.

4

As Cambridge sweltered through the yearly frenzy of finals, an initiative of the previous summer paid dividends. A merchant bank to which I had written now wrote back, offering an interview. I didn't know what merchant bankers did. I had a sketchy idea of men in back rooms, controlling Europe. The profession seemed to hold out the promise of solidity allied to a certain sexy, freewheeling capitalism that might be just the niche for my talents. I was sure I had some. The letter said there were six candidates for two jobs. The interview would take place over dinner at L'Epicure, a swanky restaurant outside Cambridge.

They'd taken a private room. The candle-lit table was set with ten places—the six candidates, all male, and four people from the bank, all men as well. I dressed in my blue suit, the one I wore on my trip to London, one that my mother had bought from Freeman's, a mail-order clothing club. The suit was made not from cotton or wool, or any of the potentially excellent synthetic fabrics, but from something that felt distinctly like cardboard: a stiff, unbending garment of surging lapels and great, flapping flares.

We started with champagne, which was followed by a

Mersault, which was followed by bottles of Châteauneuf du Pape. Foie-gras was followed by trick food, which was followed by salmon and duck. A bank guy with glasses sought my opinion about the England cricket team. A bank guy without glasses, seeing me reach for a frog's leg, used the opportunity to ask how I felt about foreign travel.

'Oh, I love it.' I explained that my father was a diplomat in Australia. No, I admitted, he hadn't yet reached ambassadorial rank.

One of the candidates I knew: Mark Greaves, from Magdalene—charming, and he'd got firsts all the way. Mature beyond his years, fleshy, a little balding, he already looked the part. A shoo-in. Another was a research student from Trinity, nervy, but with the composure not to drink too much and to say as little as possible. The competition.

Everything was going pretty well and then, while we were waiting for dessert, Mark told a joke: he glanced across the table, challenging me to tell one too. There was a brief volley of joke-telling, and I remember thinking that this had better stop now. I looked around the table, at the watchful bankers, the quietly eager guy from Trinity, cheeks gleaming. I plunged, riffing on a sketch about a dippy doctor who steals his patients' shoes. Dessert came and went. Mark recited Edward Lear. I countered with 'The Walrus and the Carpenter'. There was more champagne, brandy, cigars. Mark told a story about Polish virgins. I remembered a typically doomy one from my childhood, told to me by the gardener at my school, concerning a deaf railway engineer who had had his head knocked clean off by an Intercity 125. After the dinner was over, when I was waiting for a taxi back to the town, one of the bankers came up to me in the lobby.

'Very entertaining,' he said, languidly assured, smelling of brandy and cigars. 'Good luck.'

'Thanks,' I said and circled my hand in the air. 'Tally-ho!' Sometimes I worried: could I become my father's copy? I didn't believe so, although I couldn't have said what I was.

The Mexico wallet had been given to me by my mother, who'd had it from my stepfather, who'd bought it during his travels as an officer in the Merchant Navy during World War Two. It went with me on my trips to London, for which I was developing a ritual, my own little rumba. The blue suit was kept carefully folded along with the cheque-books and the white silk scarf in a bag in a left-luggage locker at Cambridge station. I got to the station in good time and changed there. The ticket collectors came to know me, nodding or saying hello. One had buck teeth and a shrill voice, high as a castrato. First he regarded my daily transformation with suspicion, then a wondering silence. At last he said, 'Are you a comedian?'

I'd check when a college served dinner and enter the halls of residence at that time, when rooms were likely to be empty. In case they weren't, I had a roll of Salvador Dali posters I'd offer for sale. I always knocked three times, three times for luck, knock on wood. Sometimes I had to look further than the desk. Once I was surprised by a rack of dresses in the wardrobe. I was in a girl's room. There were photographs on the bookshelf: an older woman and a man with grey hair, the mother and father, and the girl herself kneeling between two spaniels. I had a flutter of panic and guilt.

I believed in the magic of my nerve, that it was a shield that kept me safe. I became quite blasé, almost bored. I got a thrill out of selling a poster of a Dali clock to a bearded biochemistry student, having robbed the room next door. Trance-like in London, I went from bank to bank until one morning a cashier made me jump by asking quite casually: 'Would you mind signing this again?'

Be calm, I told myself, be very calm. Though I was concentrating on signing the cheque—not too slow, Christ, you're taking forever, don't muff this—I was aware of his eyes, which moved from my hand to my face and back to my hand again. When I pushed the cheque back, he stared at me openly. He knew. He compared the signatures again, holding the cheque between two fingers in both hands, and leaning down to squint at the guarantee card. 'How would you like the money, Sir?'

Most of the time it all went without a hitch. I'd say something after the cashier had checked the signature, hoping to deflect his or her attention for a second so the date wouldn't get ticked off in the calendar box at the back, and I'd be able to use the same book again that day.

British Rail shuttled me from Cambridge to Liverpool Street station, back and forth between two modes of being, and somewhere *en route* I became someone different. Lies stole trust, fraud made false coin good, theft said I could be what I pleased. I got into the part—the young businessman in his blue suit. I'd only just started, but I was eager and on the way up, confident of my accounts. I'd indicate with a smile that I was in a bit of a hurry. In the parks at lunch-time I'd still be in character. I got into a conversation with someone and said I was training to be a lawyer, working at the firm that had fired me the previous summer. I happily gave out the firm's number: 'Phone me sometime and we'll have a drink.'

London grew hot. Between one and two-thirty the parks were packed. Office boys changed into shorts, set up stumps and played cricket. Barristers snoozed beneath tents of *The Times*. A secretary kicked off her shoes and stepped out of her dress, revealing a bikini beneath. I had dreamed of such summers.

By now, I should have been able to pay back the college. Except I didn't. I couldn't. I had started spending the money—on booze, clothes and records; on suits, three of them: one black, one brown, the other a deep bottle-green, all velvet. I'd never been so flush. I took taxis and developed a taste for restaurants. I swanned about my college in my new plumage and for weeks did no laundry, throwing socks, underwear and shirts on to a daily growing heap. I bought everything new. Finals came and went, a minor interruption to the routine. When the letter came from the merchant bank, saying I hadn't got the job, that was no bother either. I simply ceased to concern myself with back rooms and Europe. I went to the King's Road and, after a fruitful morning in the banks, spent £165 on a pair of Chelsea boots, so pointy and tight I knew as soon as I got out of the shop that I'd never be able to wear them, despite the fact that they'd looked so great in the mirror, those stacked Cuban heels.

I gave them to Pete: they fitted him as if custom-made. 'Nice boots,' he said.

One day I took a white shirt from Pete's room when he wasn't there. A few days later, he asked if I had it. I said no, of course not. In some way I thought I was being accused of not just this one theft, but of all the thefts. He came up to my room and pulled the shirt out of my laundry pile.

'What's going on with you?' he said. I had nothing to say.

That same morning I was browsing in Heffers when I saw the word 'migraine' in a book. I turned the page quickly—too late. By the time I got out on to Trinity Street, I was already in what doctors call 'the haze'. My eyes and skin were tingling. My feet felt as though my shoes had been removed from them and replaced by something—cotton wool, steel wool, some fibre—that was rubbing nerves in the ends of my legs raw. I felt that a chair in the window of Belinda's coffee bar had tried to hook my eye, and that my eye would pop out of my head, which was no longer aching, but sizzling with pain. I vomited in the wash-basin as soon as I made it up the stairs to my rooms. I went on vomiting, hour after hour. This was the worst attack in years, and when at last the headache went away enough for the Migril, my prescribed drug, to send me to sleep for nearly eighteen hours, I didn't dream.

The doctors say that such attacks are connected with extremes of both stress and relaxation, moments when the self is feeling fuzzy. They are warnings. But when I finally woke up, my mind felt refreshed—scrubbed clean—and I was ready to go.

It was another hot summer night, and Harry Johnston, a friend from Downing College, just down the road from Emmanuel, had come round to see a movie with a gang of us. Harry Johnston was Glaswegian, with tight curly hair. He wore purple jeans and a black leather German army topcoat, a trophy of his father's from World War Two and an item he carried with him at all times, even during one of the hottest summers of the century. He always had more money than the rest of us. He was a drug-dealer, everyone knew. The idea occurred to me when I saw him put the key to his rooms in his coat and leave the coat on a chair at Pete's place.

The Sentinel was a horror film in which an old man, played by Burgess Meredith, stood guard over the earthly entrance to hell. The underworld's gateway was located behind a mirror in the otherwise sparsely-furnished living-room of an apartment in

New York's Greenwich Village.

I told Pete I had to take a leak, left the cinema, went back to Emmanuel, found the key to Johnston's rooms in the pocket of the leather coat and went down the street to Downing. At dusk, walking through the sandstone glow of the wide and spacious front court, I was calm and purposeful, on my way to a big score. In Johnston's rooms, I was sure there'd be cash. If I found heroin or marijuana, I'd sell it. I felt a delicious, light-headed exhilaration.

There were no drugs, Johnston was too smart for that, but there was cash (some, but nothing like the bundle I'd hoped for), a cheque-book, an American Express card and a Rolex watch. I stowed all this in a canvas bag which, on the way out, I slid beneath a bush at the entrance to the Master's Lodge, knowing I'd pick it up later. Then it was a quick sprint to Emmanuel to return the key, and I was back in the cinema before the oogie-boogies had even started coming up from hell.

The next morning, Johnston sat in Pete's room, sun-glasses on, leather coat beside him in a forlorn heap. He told how he'd been ripped off. Officers from the Flying Squad had been poking around at Downing until the wee hours, he said.

I heard this in a melting swoon. I'd thought that, because he was a drug-dealer, he wouldn't dare to call the cops. Wasn't that the way it was supposed to work, since he was a bad guy himself? And the Flying Squad! They were the élite, the crack force of the British police, with powers to move outside conventional boundaries and behave pretty much as they pleased. The image had been created by a long-running television show, *The Sweeney* (cockney rhyming slang: Sweeney Todd, Flying Squad), in which the actors John Thaw and Dennis Waterman, dressed in suits not dissimilar to my own, uttered obscenities and screeched about in souped-up Ford Granadas. Now they were looking for me.

'They said one of my friends probably did it,' Johnston said, swinging a foot. 'They wanted a list—I told them none of my friends would do something like that. I didn't want them bothering you all.'

A drug-dealer, outraged that he'd been robbed, nonetheless refused to give up the names of his friends, but he had his own reasons for not wanting The Flying Squad to poke too deeply.

Harry Johnston. I can hardly say the name. I'm ashamed. Harry Johnston was a friend. I feel the same dizzy weightlessness I did then, my mouth suddenly dry as he said: 'I've got some friends coming from the north. Business associates. They've put the word out to places where this bastard might try to sell my Rolex. We're going to do a little investigation of our own.' He grinned, showing his teeth. 'If we find him, we'll kill him.'

The IRA had launched a campaign to disrupt the run-up to the Queen's silver jubilee. A bomb went off at King's Cross. Another exploded near St Paul's Cathedral. There were few casualties, but London, already stiflingly hot, was in chaos.

I was glad I'd been in the room when Harry Johnston made his threat; I now knew to wait before trying to offload the Rolex I'd retrieved from beneath the rhododendrons at Downing. I went ahead with his Amex card and the cheque-book, however, working shops and a bank in the City when I found that the Underground had been shut because of a bomb scare at Oxford Circus. I didn't reach the West End until after midday. With cash in my pocket I thought I deserved a treat: Simpson's-in-the-Strand—rare roast beef and a bottle of claret. Smiling at an attractive American tourist, I momentarily fancied myself as a dashing fictional character: Raffles as played by David Niven, amateur cracksman, exceptional crook and perhaps the finest sportsman of his generation.

Afterwards, drunk, I sauntered along Piccadilly and stepped for a moment inside the Wren church, set back from the street, cool and spacious. After that I went into a very grand bank and let the routine take over, my hand quite steady as I wrote the cheque.

On the train back to Cambridge I realized I didn't have my briefcase. My hand flew on to the seat beside me, my eyes scanned the luggage racks, though I knew I wouldn't find it there; I'd left it in the bank, on top of the counter, shut but unlocked. There was a book in it, together with the pad on which I'd practised the signatures, and—what else? I tried to think. British Rail cushions exuded the smell of ancient dust. Sometimes I kept my own bank statements in a flap at the back of the case. If the bank spotted the passing of that particular forged cheque, found the briefcase, the pad with the signatures, and if I had left one of my own bank statements—well . . . Most considerate of you, Mr Raffles, to leave a calling card. I pictured capture, arrest, trial. I pictured trying to explain this to my mother. Oh, God.

The finest sportsman of his generation was very sick in the train lavatory.

I really didn't want to get caught. Why, then, had I left the briefcase? It was just a mistake, perhaps, but a mistake made where a high price might be paid for bad breaks. I needed a hefty slice of luck, and next day I was back at the bank within a minute or so of its opening. Two other customers were already inside, and there was a uniformed police officer standing to one side beneath the high windows. I had a few horrible seconds before I realized he was there in case of terrorists, not a Cambridge student with fraudulent tendencies.

The cashier was a woman with fair hair, cut strict around her face. She looked at me sharply when I mentioned that I rather thought I'd left my briefcase in the bank the previous day.

'I'll get the manager.'

I paced the marble floor, grinning, telling myself they couldn't know. An oak door opened and the manager popped out, an eager, balding fellow in blue pinstripes. He pranced forward with my briefcase in both hands like an offering.

'You gave us quite a fright.'

'Sorry about that.'

'We had to evacuate the bank. That was after we'd called the Bomb Squad.'

'The Bomb Squad?' I said, voice rising. 'No, really?'

This was the policeman's cue to step forward. 'This *is* your briefcase, Sir?'

'That's right.'

'Then perhaps you'd like to tell me what was inside, if you don't mind, Sir.'

I was in a bit of a fog. I said there'd been a notepad.

'Yes, we wondered about that. Found it a little . . . odd,' said the policeman. 'The signatures and all.'

'I doodle,' I said, trying to sound off-hand. 'On the train.'

'That's all right, Sir,' he said. 'People will have their foibles.

33

And was there anything else you can think of, in the briefcase, I mean?'

'Oh well, yes,' I said. 'Of course, there was a book.' There was always a book. There *is* always a book. Socks can be odd, but the book which is to be a travelling companion, that has to be perfect.

'And what book might that have been?' said the policeman.

'It was by Flann O'Brien. A hardback. A first edition of his second novel, not published until after his death. In 1967.'

'Yes, Sir,' said the policeman, round, red face all friendliness now. 'We noticed that it was a nice book. And what might the title of the novel have been, that's if you don't mind me asking?'

'It was *The Third Policeman.*'

'A little alarming, Sir, I don't mind telling you, giving everyone a scare like that.' My policeman, my first policeman, rocked to and fro on squeaky Doc Marten soles. '*Very* alarming.'

'Yes,' I said. 'I can see that. I'm really most terribly sorry.'

'The fellows from the Bomb Squad, and the lads back at the station, well . . . ' He drew out a big, white handkerchief and more or less stuffed it in his mouth, trying very hard to maintain an air of appropriate dignity. 'I don't know that I've ever seen anyone laugh so hard.'

The Queen's silver jubilee took place, despite the bombs, and Pete and I met up for a last outing. We got drunk, as did the whole of Cambridge that day. At some point, I ripped my trousers and changed into the rented tuxedo I'd be wearing that night when we planned to crash the Clare College May Ball. In the event, we bribed the college porter, who issued us with the little orange discs that said we were bulletproof.

Once inside, Pete was very much the *flâneur* in his suit of bottle-green velvet. I competed by signing for seven or eight bottles of champagne under the name the Rev. Raymond Hockley, who happened to be the chaplain of our own college. It wasn't long before we were rumbled. Five beefy boat-club types came up and demanded to know which of us was the Rev. Raymond Hockley. We had to make a run for it, across the bridge, between the torches that flickered and hissed on the path beside the Fellows' Garden and up the high iron gate at the back of the college.

I paused for a moment at the top, fifteen feet off the ground. The river gave off an earthy summer smell—mushrooms in a bag. Soon I'd be walking back through the town in the light of dawn, kicking my heels on a misty summer morning. Cambridge was over, and I promised myself I'd never have anything to do with crime again. Ahead were trees and shadows, a road, the ominous bulk of the University Library.

I jumped down to the other side.

5

Weeks sweltered by. The summer persisted, stiflingly hot. I sat in the garden, re-reading the first four cantos of *Don Juan*. My mother and stepfather were in the kitchen, peeping at me over the tops of their newspapers. 'What do you expect?' I heard my stepfather say through the kitchen window. 'He's just a loafer.'

I had returned to my mother's house in Yorkshire—to do what? To moon about. From our local bookshop I stole a first edition of *The Four Quartets*. I returned for the beautiful Collins first edition of *Byron: the Years of Fame* by Peter Quenell. Wimbledon was another drug.

I thought I might write a novel and bought notebooks and plenty of sharp, new pencils. I recorded the opening of *The Four Quartets* in my own voice and played it back to myself each night over the stereo in my bedroom.

> *Time present and time past*
> *Are both perhaps present in time future,*
> *And time future contained in time past.*
> *If all time is eternally present*
> *All time is unredeemable.*

My stepsister came to stay. I was stretched in front of the television, watching the golf, while she and Denise Robinson, a pretty neighbour, talked about a party they were going to that weekend.

'It's in the Lake District,' said my stepsister. 'It's going to be absolutely *wonderful*.'

Denise Robinson was from a rich family who lived up on The Grove, a private road opposite our house. She told my stepsister that they could drive to the party: she had the car; her parents were away—on holiday, on a Greek island, Mallorca, the Costa del . . . somewhere.

As Tom Watson holed out from the sand with a miraculous nine-iron swish, the idea soared up out of the blue: the Robinsons' house was empty. I would rob the Robinsons. As soon as I had the thought, I realized I had no choice: I would have to rob them. I was delighted, afraid.

That night, I laid out my costume on the bed: dark jeans, black T-shirt, a pair of Adidas trainers. From the attic I pulled down a pair of beige canvas bags. In my mother's dressing-table, I found a pair of thin, black leather gloves. They were a tight fit and smelled faintly of perfume. The next morning, Friday, I walked up The Grove. The Robinsons' house was built in blackened Yorkshire sandstone, a big, square building with white shutters. Ivy crept up the left side, and an immaculate lawn rolled away from the house down to tall, stone gateposts with dragons on top, wings outstretched. The house and grounds stood back behind a line of sheltering elms. The house looked solid and prosperous. It looked as though it had many treasures inside.

I returned in the evening to get a sense of how the house would be in the dark. Along The Grove itself, there were only a few street lamps; in front of the house, there was a stretch, about a hundred yards, bordered on both sides by trees that leaned towards each other to form a dark canopy. It was entirely black, like the entrance to a rabbit hole. I could hear my feet, but not see them. I stood still, taking in the night smells of roses and lavender, and the whisper of foliage overhead. A bat brushed against my face. So much for their radar.

That evening, I sat in the living-room with *Don Juan*. Juan had met Julia, 'charming, chaste and twenty-three,' and had 'unutterable thoughts'. Her husband, Don Alfonso, justly suspicious, searched every nook and cranny of the bedroom, except under the bedclothes where Juan lay hiding, all but suffocated between Julia's legs—until his tell-tale pair of shoes gave him away. While Alfonso rushed to get his sword, Juan had to fly! Down the back stairs—handy.

I thought of Denise Robinson. As she'd left with my stepsister, she had given me a little smile. She was the kind of girl I wished to fall in love with. What if she were to be in the house, waiting, when I robbed it? In bed that night I was tucked up with unutterable thoughts of my own.

But when Saturday came around, there was a problem. My mother and stepfather announced that they weren't going out.

But you *always* go out on a Saturday night, I told them.

'Not tonight,' my mother said, obviously in a foul mood.

I slumped in front of the television. I pouted and sulked. I sighed. It wasn't until I'd thrown a full-scale tantrum, turning red in the face and declaring that this said it all—I was never allowed any time to myself in this house—that my mother gave in.

Smiling, I kissed her on the cheek. I helped my stepfather on with his coat. And then pushed them out of the house. I stood in the road, waving, until the red tail-lights of the Rover disappeared. In minutes I was in costume. I had the two canvas bags, one folded inside the other, along with a torch, some old newspapers and a roll of inch-wide Sellotape. I walked up The Grove, through the rabbit hole, between the stone gates with the threatening statuary. I was breathing hard. Was I really going through with this? Of course, it was written, fated, but would I actually do it? I went around the side of the house and tried the back door, just in case—locked. No matter: I had my plan.

I hadn't counted on the flower-beds: wide flower-beds, thick with rose bushes. Lovely to sniff, not so easy to wade among with the canvas bags held high above my head. And when at last I reached the window, I found that the stone sill was much higher than it had appeared from the road—nearly level with my shoulders. I had to balance the canvas bag on it while hoisting myself up after, taking care not to knock the bag off. I stood there, side on, pressed against the window pane, one foot in front of the other as if I were on a tightrope. I felt exposed, as well as stupid and frightened: in danger of nose-diving into the bushes, or, if I pressed too hard on the glass, tumbling through it into the house.

I reached into the bag for the Sellotape, ripped off a few

strips with my teeth, criss-crossed the window, then smashed the glass with the end of the torch. I'd seen a burglar do this on television. I was surprised that it worked, but then, why not? The glass came away with a sound like crunching sugar.

I found the latch, raised the sash, slid over, pulling the bag after me. I was inside.

There was an impression of silence, of space, of a thick, pressing darkness that—even though pierced by me a moment before—was already settling back all around. Somewhere there was the tick of a clock, counting time at a much slower beat than once a second. Or so it seemed. Everything was different, as if I were in Captain Nemo's vessel and this the view from the bottom of the sea. I felt the empty house with my nerve ends: old stone surrounding an atmosphere that asked me, politely, to disturb it as little as possible, even if I was a thief. The house felt alive, not unwelcoming.

After a few minutes, my eyes grew accustomed to the darkness. I sensed the proportions of the room. It was big, with dark patches and doorways that I imagined must lead to other rooms.

I turned on the torch. Its beam discovered a fireplace and a mantelpiece and a glinting carriage-clock with decorative doodads on top. A mirror flashed my light back at me. As I moved the torch, new objects came up out of the darkness. A little round coffee table with dimpled edges. A three-piece suite. To my left, there was another room, disappearing around a corner. The torch created one half of a dining-table and the ribbed backs of two or three chairs. A standard lamp sprang up, with a tasselled shade. I turned off the torch and waited again. Everything had a glow, as if the objects themselves were a source of light. There was no moon.

I took down the carriage-clock, the doodads, and wrapped them in newspaper so they wouldn't break when I put them in the bag. I hadn't thought about *what* I was going to steal. A house contained an infinity of objects. Which ones were valuable? I entered the dining-room, and shiny silver things—candlesticks, a cigarette box, a fruit dish—caught my attention, a hero stumbling on a dragon's hoard.

I made my feet quiet, stealing with an almost tender care.

From the dining-room, I entered a much thicker darkness and had to turn on the torch again. This was the hallway, high, with a wood parquet floor and wood panels all around. A staircase was on my left, wide and carpeted. Light gleamed from glass in picture frames. On the landing was a double-window with stained glass.

I left behind the one bag I'd filled and took the stairs two at a time, swinging myself around on the banister at the landing. I was upstairs. A door was open.

This was a bedroom, the master bedroom, where Mr and Mrs Robinson slept. The double bed had a plain walnut headboard. There was a chest of drawers and a dressing-table with a mirror that bounced back light. Mainly, there were smells: of make-up and perfume, Brylcreem, mothballs and musty clothes, of sleep. The curtains were drawn. The impression was of an old-fashioned cosiness, as of a room lived in by people much older than myself. I'd been in this room before, though; it was my mother and stepfather's.

I swept up the silver dressing-table set. A case of jewels went straight into the bag. Another case, decorated with mother-of-pearl, sat on a lace doily. Inside were rings, earrings, chains and brooches all caught up together in a knot.

I returned to the landing and entered another room, neat and neutral-smelling—the guest-room. The curtains were open, and I was careful not to let the beam of the torch strike the darkened window-panes. Here I am, I thought, I'm a burglar, being a burglar.

The next room was Denise Robinson's. The fragrances were lighter, more delicate. A window was open a few inches, letting in a breeze and the smells of the night. The bed was made. A teddy bear and hand-stitched cushions were on one side of it. There was a bookshelf with many of the same books my stepsister had: *Jane Eyre, Gone with the Wind*, two or three by R. F. Delderfield, *Rogue Herries* by Hugh Walpole. There was another jewellery case and, on a table, a vase, shapely, made from glass that was opaque and grainy. I held Denise Robinson's pillow to my face and smelt it. I thought I might like to stay here forever

How long was I there? I had to fight against the wonderful, strange feeling of being comfortable in a place so familiar that it could have been home. I had started out well enough downstairs, but up here, in the bedrooms, I'd been thrown.

Winking glass caught my attention as I was on my way down. I turned the torch.

The picture, huge, in a gilt frame above the landing, was of a stag, side on, attention caught—looking straight at me. Antlers forked upwards to the top of the frame. In the background were a river, misty woodlands and a snow-capped mountain range. The stag as proud sovereign.

It was a Landseer, not an original, at least I didn't think so, although it might have been for all I knew or know, but a copy in oils old enough to be worth something. I ran down the stairs, put the second bag alongside the first, with the torch on top, and then returned and stood beneath the picture. With my arms stretched out wide, I could just reach the frame at its sides— good. I stood up on tiptoe and lifted, trying to get the picture off its hooks, but it didn't budge. I took a deep breath and tried again, heaving: a mistake, because this time the picture did come away, all of a sudden, and it was so much heavier than expected that I staggered backwards. I hit something, the banister, which creaked and seemed for a moment sure to break, dropping me fifteen feet on to the hallway floor with the picture on top of me, in which position I imagined myself being found by the returning Robinsons: thief crushed by Landseer.

The banister held, but the frame then slid through my hands and came down on the stairs with an almighty thump. I was forced to jump forward quickly to keep the picture from then sliding away down the stairs. I stood there, panting.

I saw the problem. The frame: it had been absurd to try to take the picture still inside it. Struggling down The Grove with this great thing—impossible. And conspicuous? Not much. I had to get the canvas out of the frame and roll it up carefully, the way I'd seen Kirk Douglas do in that movie about Vincent Van Gogh.

The painting itself was the valuable thing, correct?

I laid the picture flat on the landing. I nipped back down for the torch and a knife. I imagined I could cut out the canvas from the back, but once I turned the frame over, I realized it was impossible: the picture was secured by wood and layers of canvas. There were scrawled auction marks in chalk and the name and address of a framer in Leeds. The date at the top was 1892: my knife merely added a few ineffectual scratches.

I turned the picture over again—the stag gazed at me with a curious eye—and brought down the end of the torch and cracked the glass, my idea now being to remove it and get the canvas out from the front. I then stood the frame up on its edge and jiggled, expecting the glass to fall away, but nothing happened. I gave the glass another whack, a good one this time. A piece of glass the size of my thumbnail plopped out on to the carpet.

I took off my gloves. I ran my hands over the shattered surface of the glass—uneven now, with lots of sharp edges—and attacked the splinters, pulling them out one by one. Somehow I contrived not to cut myself and when I'd cleared away a small area of canvas I put my gloves on again, easing loose the jagged pieces, tugging them away. It was slow going, and I'd been at it a little while, when something slid inside my concentration, a sound. I hadn't noticed it before. I moved the picture carefully to one side and stepped down the stairs. I stood, my head spinning, in the vastness of the hall, trying to locate the source. It wasn't a ringing, more of a suppressed buzzing, as if someone were trying to shut up a phone by smothering it with a cushion.

I'd assumed that the Robinsons would have an alarm, but since it hadn't gone off when I'd smashed the window, I'd pushed the thought away, supposing either that they didn't have one after all or that it had been circumvented by my sheer burglary skill. I hadn't considered the possibility that there would be an alarm that wouldn't go off at first, that there would be a *delay*.

I asked myself why would anyone do that, install an alarm with a delay? Obviously the thing had been tripped the moment I'd broken in, so why hadn't it started ringing then? Perhaps, I concluded, because the alarm was connected to the police station, where it had been ringing for a while already.

My head itched. My sweat was cold. My hands were damp, my armpits clammy. I went liquid. My insides too: fear, anger at myself for not having seen the possibility, even a little outrage at the deceit, the fact that someone had worked out a trap—all these were sloshing about. I could see every line on the parquet floor. I wished to escape by sinking down into them.

The light filtering through the stained-glass window on the landing seemed much brighter. Was that the beam of a police car? At that moment the muted buzzing stopped. There was a brief and eerie silence before the alarm started going off, full blast. It clanked and then it thundered. The floor quivered with the force of it, an alarm clearly designed to make the intruder flee, now, forcing him into his car and down The Grove, where he'd meet the police coming up the other way.

I didn't have a car. I didn't panic. I saw what I had to do. I collected the two bags, the torch, my things, and went to the front door. I had to put down the bags while I fiddled with bolts and locks. But soon I was back out into the night, trotting down the path as fast as I dared with the two bags dragging at my arms. The night was warm and muggy, and still no moon. Here, outside, the deafening clank of the alarm seemed muted again. What with the big lawns and gardens, and the trees surrounding them, there was a chance the neighbours might not have heard it.

I got to the gates where the dragons stood guard and, instead of turning left down The Grove, I turned in the opposite direction, walking up the hill for a hundred yards or so. I climbed a flimsy wire fence into a field and pulled the bags through after. Far below, at the bottom of the valley, car headlights meandered along beside the river. I knew a place to hide the bags. Then I'd walk up the hill back to our house, maybe even stop for a pint on the way. Between me and where I had to get was an area that was perhaps half a mile wide. During the day there would be a herd of Jersey cows. But at night? I saw nothing. In the distance I heard sirens. I walked down into the pitch-dark field.

'Guess what?' my stepsister said. She was back from the Lake District. 'The Robinsons were burgled at the weekend.' We were eating breakfast. I had marmaladed toast in one paw and my nose in the sports pages of the *Daily Telegraph*. All that summer the West Indies were handing England another pasting.

'The house was ransacked,' she said.

My stepfather looked up from his own newspaper. 'Disgraceful,' he said.

I took another bite. This was unfair: the house had not been ransacked. I'd been very careful about that, until the Landseer.

'They got away with thousands of pounds' worth of stuff,' she said. The Flying Squad had been there most of the day and all of the previous night after Denise had got back. They'd collected evidence and dusted the house for prints. According to them, the 'job' was one of a series that had been 'pulled' in the area.

The Flying Squad had been called in on my account again. I stared at my stepsister. I'd always found her sexy. I was feeling smug. You think you know who I am, I thought, but I know better—by day that loafer with the Cambridge degree, but come the night . . . Zorro.

I swelled with a daft glory, pleased that my work had been mistaken for that of a professional. I spread marmalade on another luxuriantly buttered piece of toast.

It was only when I was in my room that something else my stepsister had said sunk in. The Flying Squad had taken fingerprints. All at once I had a clear memory of myself, on the landing, removing my gloves. I was all liquid again. Jubilation turned to fear, and I had to sit down to wait for it to pass, but it didn't, not quite. It became an anxiety that lingered for the rest of the day and then the next. I don't know why I was so worried. The Flying Squad had nothing to compare them against. My fingerprints had never been taken. I had no criminal record.

I fidgeted and snapped. What if I'd been seen?

Gradually, the anxiety diminished, although when I went to collect the bags from where I'd left them, under the bushes that decorated a small roundabout in the middle of a council estate, I did hang about for what seemed like hours, fearful that the real-life Sweeney counterparts of Thaw and Waterman were lurking nearby in their souped-up Granadas. At last I called up the nerve. There was nobody. I had a hard job hefting the bags back.

In my room, I laid out the haul: two silver cigarette-boxes, a brass carriage-clock, four matching silver candlesticks, a set of silver cutlery in a box lined with red plush, a silver sweet dish, an opaque glass vase in the style of Lalique. There was a Sony cassette player and amplifier. From the jewellery boxes I pulled out two amethyst rings, a pair of pearl stud earrings, a single-strand pearl necklace. The pearls were real, as I discovered when I rolled them against my teeth and found their texture slightly abrasive, gritty—a trick I'd learned from a James Bond novel.

I consulted a little book my stepfather had about gold and silver hallmarks and was delighted to discover that the silver candelabra dated from York in the nineteenth century and might be worth a lot. In one of the other jewellery boxes, I found gold: three thin gold chains and a chunky gold bracelet with twenty-three charms. There was a gold stagecoach, I remember; a gold fleur-de-lis, a gold lion and a gold cat with little chips of emerald for eyes—one charm, I realized, for each of Denise Robinson's birthdays.

Suddenly I wanted to make amends, to confess—or maybe not that, but at least to pack the stuff back up and leave it on the Robinsons' doorstep. But they would have been insured up to the neck, I told myself. By now they'd have reported the theft and it would be inconvenient if I started monkeying with the process. They might even lose out.

Gold! I cackled like Fagin.

There was a knock on the door. 'Rich, are you all right?'

It was my mother. The silence hummed.

'You're talking to yourself,' she said.

I threw a tartan travel rug in the air and watched it settle over my treasures. 'I'm fine, Mum, thanks,' I said. 'I'll be down in a minute.'

6

I couldn't dispose of the loot in Yorkshire. London was the obvious place, and also the obvious place to live. A friend had set me up with a cushy number, doing blurbs for videos—new-fangled things in 1977. And there was the prospect of writing for *Time Out*, *New Society* and the *New Statesman*.

As soon as I got off the train, I took the tube to Queensway, where I'd stayed the previous summer while working for the law firm that fired me, and checked into the first hotel I found. The room had no toilet or shower, and was so tiny that there was barely room to stand up between the bed and the wash-basin. Twelve pounds a night, in advance, but I was thrilled—the metropolitan life.

I'd always experienced London as an ordeal. Before my summer of bad cheques, I knew London from trips with my mother and stepfather to see West End farces or the *Black and White Minstrel Show*—or with my father: once, when I was eight, I'd lain awake in a room I was sharing with him in a hotel near Regent's Park while he argued with a prostitute over the price of a service she was about to provide. I'd sneaked away from the school to see Stanley Kubrick's *A Clockwork Orange* on the first day of its release at the big Warner cinema in Leicester Square, and for a while Pete had loaned me his London. Now my own London was waiting. All I had to do was invent it. I walked up teeming Queensway past the tube station and into the green of Hyde Park. It was still light, I had a book in my hand, people were out with their dogs or just strolling, and I was happy. In London I could be whatever character I chose.

The next morning I joined the British Library at the British Museum, an ugly building, but one designed by the same architect who'd done the façade at Emmanuel, a late nineteenth-century addition, and so it felt like home. There was the promise of a routine: up early, walk through the falling leaves on Holland Park Avenue, up Notting Hill Gate, straight down Oxford Street to Bloomsbury. London was golden. At the Museum a uniformed official checked my briefcase and my reader's ticket, a laminated plastic card with a photo.

I took a place in the circular reading room where every sound—a chair being slid back, a book thumped shut—flew up into the domed ceiling, where some of it was absorbed before being bounced back with a gentle belch; the reading room was a stomach in which to absorb learning, a chamber filled with the mysterious rumbles of terribly polite indigestion. The chairs were heavy and solid, backed with blue. The catalogues were ranged in a smaller circle at the room's hub, enormous volumes where the titles and shelf information were pasted on little slips.

Usually I went to the North Library. As the day wore on, the room's oblong lamps enclosed me in a golden light that seemed to have been spun from some fibre, while above there was darkness—a vast protective space. I wrote out for the umpteenth time my new novel's opening sentence.

'Crossing the Strand was an adventure—Heywood felt like a mountaineer as he walked into the pub to ask his father for a loan.'

I took some of the better-looking stuff from the Robinsons' to a jeweller on High Holborn. He was an old man in a hairy tweed suit, his polka-dot bow-tie set a little skew, like a propeller about to start spinning. He inspected the gold charms on the bracelet and, one by one, the hallmarks on the four silver candlesticks, and then he offered me eighty-two pounds. It was an oddly precise and astoundingly small sum. I said I'd been thinking more along the lines of two hundred pounds (actually I'd been thinking along the lines of far more than that), and the old man's face took on a little angry shine. I took the eighty-two.

Afterwards, I felt outrage: I'd been cheated. I'd risked so much for so little. I thought about rushing back in to snatch what I could, or breaking in that night.

I rode the Underground without a ticket. My thoughts strayed aimlessly. I found it hard to fix on anything. In the street I couldn't imagine what went on behind faces. Everyone seemed hard.

In a panic I got a job at the local Wimpy, spent a day sweeping floors, couldn't bear to go back the next day and so didn't get paid. I thought about going on the dole, but no, the dole was for people worse than the lofty view I had of myself. It was clear that I was going to run into money trouble. I had already written two reviews for *Time Out* and an observation piece for *New Society*: neither had paid me yet.

I forced myself to be busy, to keep moving, the next day marching through the rain in an RAF greatcoat which my mother had dyed black and which now began to lose its borrowed colour. Dye trickled down my neck, dripped on to the floor of Poole's, the famous second-hand bookshop at 84 Charing Cross Road, where I went in the hope of spotting things I could sell on. One morning I got *Lolita* and two V. S. Naipauls—*Miguel Street* and *A House for Mr Biswas*—for less than three pounds. At a specialist first-edition shop the proprietor offered twenty-five, more than I was expecting.

I never had such luck at Poole's again.

At lunch-time, I left my briefcase behind in the British Library and walked around the National Gallery, telling myself I was learning about pictures. One day I went the other way and stopped outside the Royal Academy of Dramatic Arts to see if anyone I knew from Cambridge featured in the production stills outside. In Dillons, the big university bookshop, I mooched around in the second-hand department and at the tables near the front with the new publications. I walked out with the Duckworth reprint of an Evelyn Waugh travel book, *Labels*, under my arm.

I felt them before I saw them, right between the shoulders. I was being followed, two people, a man and a woman, dressed in bulky parkas—store detectives. If I made a run for it I could get away, down Gower Street and into the back entrance of the Museum. I could lose myself there. I pictured two store detectives trying to get past security at the entrance to the Reading Room.

Or I could walk around the corner, back into Dillons, through the side entrance, dump the book, and, even if they caught up with me, deny everything. That would work too.

It was a cool, grey day. Everything seemed crisp and bright. A cab came towards me with its yellow light on and stopped at a zebra crossing. I didn't move, I didn't try to move, I didn't want to move. The paving stones were huge beneath my feet.

At Tottenham Court Road police station I was put in front of a white board with black measuring marks. A flashbulb popped. Handcuffs still on, my fingers were smeared over a black inky tablet and then pressed on to a printed sheet of paper—a box for each finger. I was left alone in an interview room.

I wanted this to be over. I'd been caught, I wasn't pretending I'd not been caught, I was offering myself up for punishment and I wished it wouldn't take so long. I'd been marched back into Dillons, a store detective on either side. People had looked at me with curiosity, scorn, a gladness they weren't in my shoes. The male store detective, a lanky Iranian, had made me a cup of too-sweet tea in the manager's office. The manager himself, pink in the face, asked me how many other books I had stolen, then, eh?

The police interview room had grey lino, bilious yellow walls and a scarred metal desk in the middle. I'd been told to sit on a plastic chair with spindly legs that wobbled. I waited, convinced that my fingerprints were being cross-checked and that a Flying Squad detective was about to burst through the door and ask what I knew about a certain house near Bradford, belonging to the—ah—Robinsons.

At last a door opened, and a white-haired giant of a man came in, a sergeant, lugging a typewriter so enormous that I thought he was perhaps the only one in the station strong enough to carry it. He laid it gently on the desk, rolled in a form and, making it clear that his own remedy for boredom was to take everything at a slow, slow pace, asked me my name, my date of birth, my present address, my phone number. He had a soft, Irish voice. He met each of my replies with a weary stare, then looked down and picked out the letters with agonizing slowness. He didn't ask if I'd committed any other crimes. I'd have confessed to everything, anything. Instead, when he finished, he said, 'You silly, silly man.'

The cell smelled powerfully of disinfectant. There was a mattress, but no blanket or pillow, and a toilet without a seat or a handle. There was a funny little dimple in the steel door where the peephole was on the other side. There was a single bulb, not on at the moment, protected by a thick wire-mesh. At the far end of the cell, light filtered weakly through a grille of opaque glass. There was a constant muffled patter, footsteps. The Tottenham Court Road pavement was only a few feet above.

I sat on the bed, determined to take in every detail. They'd taken away my pens, watch and wallet, and sealed them in a plastic bag. They'd taken away my shoe laces and my belt. This was all very interesting, I thought.

Graffiti were all over the walls: GUNNERS RULE; FUCK TOTTENHAM YIDS; FUCK THE LAW; FUCK ALL COPPERS; FUCK, FUCK, FUCK.

I'd be out in an hour or two, the sergeant had said, as soon as they'd checked my address. I'd be released on bail and would have to report to Bow Street Magistrate's Court in the morning. I was in bright form. I sat on the edge of the bed and examined the tiles on the wall opposite me, counting the cracks.

I recited poetry and scenes from movies, hummed the theme tune from the *Mr Ed* television show, made up dialogue in my head. It started getting dark, and I worried that I might not get out in time to nip back to the Museum and collect my stuff.

Soon, the grey light of the grille had disappeared. This was no longer interesting. 'Silly man,' the Irish sergeant had said. 'Silly'—that was right, all right; 'man' erred on the side of flattery. I was frightened, cold in the dark, and when I came to the door and shouted, no one came. I thought the sergeant might have left an order that this was to happen: give the Cambridge boy a scare.

'Turn on the light!'

I thought at least someone would hear me in one of the adjoining cells. There was nothing; it must have been a slow day for crime in the West End.

'TURN ON THE LIGHT, YOU FUCKERS.'

I was kept in the dark for only ten hours. I say 'only'. No one came or went. *Were* there any other cells? I began to think I was being held in a special insulated tank. I shouted until I was hoarse. I wept. People up on the pavement must have heard and, though I was ashamed, knowing I must have made a sad display, I didn't stop.

At Bow Street the magistrate's demeanour suggested that he was shocked, frankly shocked, that I wasn't up there for trying to nab a policeman's helmet on Boat Race night. He sat high above me on his bench. He had a pink shiny face and silver half-moon spectacles over which his eyes peered at mine as he asked me how I wished to plead.

'Guilty.'

'*Guilty?*' he said, as if I were trying to trick him.

'Yes, Sir, guilty.'

'So you went to—ah—Cambridge, where you read philosophy and, and . . . *law*.' He gazed at me over those glittery half-moons. This was obviously another trick. 'And you work for the mmm *Time Out* and the *New* . . . yes, and the *New* . . .'

At the front sat a reporter from the local paper. Worth a story? I hoped not. In my statement I'd needlessly told all this,

49

storing up my present humiliation.

The magistrate went on, 'You've had lots more opportunities than most of the people I see and now it seems you're in danger of turning yourself into a thoroughly bad lot. What do you have to say for yourself?'

I said I was very sorry, and it would never happen again, Sir.

With a heavy sigh he examined the evidence, the book I'd tried to steal. This perked him up.

'Evelyn Waugh? When I bought this book in 1938 it cost me three shillings and sixpence.' He gave an eager look around, but no one laughed. No bother: he'd been practising law and bad jokes for forty years.

'Fined seventy-five pounds.'

By the time I left the court another defendant was up in the box, a tramp who'd got himself arrested so he could spend the night in jail with a roof over his head, and to whose company the magistrate was wearily accustomed.

'Do you really suppose,' he asked the tramp, 'that the state can go on supporting you forever in this manner?'

The huge courtroom doors banged shut, cutting off the tramp's reply. I walked across the black-and-white marble lozenges of the lobby floor. There was a marble bust set in a recess of the wall, a likeness of Henry Fielding, novelist-turned-magistrate. It was a waterfall, drenching me with relief.

I'd deserved what I got: a criminal record, which now disqualified me from ever pursuing a career at law. It made me both angry—that it was in other people's power to judge me so—and rather happy. I promised myself that never again, ever, would I find myself where I'd just been.

I strolled into the bright chill November air, strolled along Long Acre, up Charing Cross Road, Tottenham Court Road, strolled into Dillons and out again with another book under my arm, this time a first edition of *Dead Babies* by Martin Amis, the one with the picture of him on the back of the jacket, smoking a fag and looking like Mick Jagger. I strolled back, taking the route I'd expected to take the day before, into the British Museum's back entrance.

I had to prove that I wasn't beaten.

GRANTA

STEVE PYKE
WHY AM I RICH?

'What do I attribute my success to? Being a good listener and striving to succeed in the pursuit of excellence.'

John Madejski, fifty-two. Publisher. Estimated wealth £140 million.

'I believe in meritocracy and benevolent capitalism.
Political idealism and the preservation of our cultural heritage
are also high priorities in my mind.'

Christopher Moran, forty-six. Financier. Estimated wealth £150
million.

'Respect the privilege of money and never forget that only real risk can provide true reward.'

Matthew Harding, forty. Insurance tycoon and director of Chelsea Football Club. Estimated wealth £145 million.

'I attribute my success to understanding consumers' needs and providing well-designed products at the right price.'

Gulu Lalvani, fifty-four. Chairman, Binatone Electronics International. Estimated wealth £25 million.

'I'm successful because I'm brilliant and I'm wealthy because
I'm successful.'

Bill Gredley, sixty-one. Property developer and racehorse owner.
Estimated wealth £80 million.

'Lord Palumbo doesn't want to appear in your magazine, but I
don't suppose there's anything we can do about it.'

Lord Palumbo, fifty-eight. Property developer. Estimated wealth
£80 million.

'I think I have the best job around . . .
Success comes from focusing in on what you really like and are
good at—not challenging every random thing.'

Bill Gates, thirty-nine. Chairman and co-founder of Microsoft.
Estimated wealth, $9.35 billion.

GRANTA

IAN HAMILTON
THE TROUBLE WITH MONEY

A·ALVAREZ • Dan
Jacobson •SIMON GRAY
EDNA O'BRIEN ~~~~
Thomas Hinde• CLIVE
JAMES• Roy Fuller •
Christopher Ricks ~~
GEORGE STEINER• Peter
Porter•MICHAEL FRIED
DOUGLAS DUNN• John
Gross •RUSSELL DAVIES
MELVYN BRAGG •Shena Mackay
Patricia Highsmith•EDWARD
PYGGE and many others
Edited by IAN HAMILTON

Did you know that a hundred-gram jar of Nescafé filled with 1p coins buys two packets of Benson and Hedges? Did you know that a two-litre flagon of Paul Masson burgundy filled with 2p coins buys three regular-size bottles of Safeway's claret? Did you know that a Steradent tube filled with 10p coins buys just over one-and-a-half bottles of Night Nurse?

Perhaps you didn't. Why should you? Why should I? And yet I dote on such statistics; rarely do they fail to cheer me up. I can be twenty grand down at the bank, the tax on my heels and a heap of nasties on the mat, but for some reason the spectacle of my three-quarters-full-and-rising coffee jar gives me a sense of high accomplishment, a feeling that I've licked, have nearly licked, will lick the system. As long as those bronze chiplets continue to pile up, I tell myself, I'm not out of the game. I am a saver.

There are, of course, other ways of saving. For these, though, you need to be 'in funds'. For example, you can hide a fiver in a coat you never wear, or tuck a tenner in a sock that's had its day. The idea is that you'll forget about these minor-league deposits. After all, what's fifteen pounds when you are packing a new wad? And then, when things turn rough again and you just happen to be trying on old coats and socks—you know, the way one does when things turn rough—there they will be: salvation, a new start! The loopholes in this strategem are self-evident, and it's not one that I recommend for workaday survival. But it does have some poetic substance. It makes money seem like magic. As with the coffee jars, although more chancily, it tells you that you're still in with a chance.

Childish stuff, you may well think, and you'd probably be right. But for some of us, it has become the stuff of life—the stuff, that is, of literary life. Knowing how many days pass between a final notice and a cut-off, knowing how much time you

Ian Hamilton began the *Review* in 1962 while still a student at Oxford. The *New Review*—a monthly publication of poetry, fiction, book reviews and essays—was launched in 1974, initially supported by an Arts Council grant of £1,000 per issue. Opposite: the writer Richard Boston, on Old Compton Street in Soho, advertising the first issue of the new magazine.

gain with a carefully-phrased 'WAFDA pdc' (post-dated cheque on which the 'words and figures don't agree'), knowing the phone codes for Northampton, Worthing and Southend ('A friendly-sounding fellow called. Could you please ring him back?'): such information is the small change of a life that's sometimes financed by small change. And you can easily get hooked on your own expertise. A sudden access of riches can induce a sense of desolation. What to do with all this know-how, all this *change*?

Back in the early sixties, when I first started out, insolvency spelt glamour. It was OK to be broke—more than OK, since money was well-known to be the super-foe of books. It was Mammon v. the Muses: take your pick. In those days, if a writer owned up to caring about money, he was instantly branded a dud. 'He's got a *what*? A mortgage? Well, I have to say I always had my doubts. I mean, his line-breaks did seem a bit *arbitrary*.' The avowed aim was to treat money rather as money seemed likely to treat us: with altitudinous contempt.

There was, of course, an easy fraudulence in this, since none of us was poor—well, not *poor* poor—but we weren't ready then to spot it. We intended to set up as 'sons of literature' (in Dr Johnson's noble phrase). Had not literature itself decreed that we should not make friends with Mammon? The modern texts we had learned to decipher for our school exams were all to do with tensions between money and non-money. For A-level English I studied *The Waste Land* and *Howards End* and I still have the actual books I worked from. The margins of each resemble a roster of sports fixtures: 'inner life v. outer', 'money values v. culture values', 'Wilcoxes (money) v. Schlegels (sensibility)', 'Mr Eugenides (merchant) v. hyacinth girl (spiritual illumination)'. With the Forster, I am glad to see, there is the odd underlining or question mark, as if I might now and then have been trying to work out something for myself: 'To trust people is a luxury only the wealthy can indulge' is marked with a combative 'Trust you!' The overall impression, though, is of tame capitulation to the belief that works of art are like messages in bottles from some dire cultural shipwreck—a wreck caused, of course, by money. As students, it was our clear duty to man life-rafts and set sail.

There was, then, a near-priestly kind of romance in the idea that a high-purposed literary career would be profitless, at least in terms of cash. Here was the Thorny Way, the way of deprivation. And for a period, I went along with this, nose in the air. At the same time, though, I knew I could handle only so much deprivation. That painting of the dead Chatterton sprawled on his pallet never made me want to be like him. Nor, come to that, did I want to be like Keats and Shelley. And the then-recent cult of Dylan Thomas left me cold. Thomas's whipped-dog act when he was cadging the price of his next drink seemed horribly demeaning. And look at the way he carried on when he had swallowed his next drink: all that intoning-from-above, that bardic blethering. He too was like a priest. He seemed to think the world owed him a living.

With attitudes like these, I was clearly in something of a fix. On the one hand, it was contemptible to have a mortgage; on the other, a fellow ought to be able to pay for the next round. What did that leave? It left the Cobbled Way, the way of compromise. And my compromise was to start up a small poetry magazine. How better to reconcile the importunities of art and commerce?

In those days—this was 1962—I was much fired by the early letters of Ezra Pound, the ones that deal with his efforts on behalf of magazines like the *Little Review* and *Poetry (Chicago)*. Pound was a superb backs-to-the-wall businessman, it seemed to me. An enemy of money, or of 'money-values', he recognized yet did not flinch from money's power. He was brilliant at locating and tapping likely sources of largesse. With him, though, there was none of Thomas's spare-a-penny-guv self-humbling. His benefactors were usually left feeling grateful: such was the high vehemence of his belief in the world-altering potential of his cause. And they were even more grateful when Pound from time to time slipped them a Joyce worksheet or a drawing by Gaudier-Brzeska. Pound never made the mistake of despising his money-men. He treated them like converts. I remember being mightily impressed by his retort to his two arty-crafty co-editors on the *Little Review*, when they spoke scornfully of the millionaire John Quinn. It was Quinn's money that guaranteed the magazine's survival. Pound wrote to them:

Re: Quinn, remember. Tis he who hath bought the
pictures: tis he who both getteth me an American
publisher and smacketh the same with rods; tis he who
sendeth me the Spondos Oligos, which is by interpretation
the small tribute or spondoolicks wherewith I do pay my
contributors, WHEREFORE is my heart softened toward the
said J.Q. and he in mine eyes can commit nothing
heinous.

This seemed to me to strike precisely the right note. For
Pound, the trouble with money was that it kept bad company.
With his help, it would learn to make new friends. At the time, I
didn't pay much attention to the economic theories of Pound's
later years, nor did I brood deeply on *Hugh Selwyn Mauberley*, in
which he calls himself 'wrong from the start . . . born in a half-
savage country, out of date.' What mattered to me then—or so I
said—was the man's energy and style, his fiercely-held conviction
that money could be made to see the light.

Cultural high-mindedness allied with pecuniary cunning:
well, why not? I set up shop—first of all with the *Review* and
later with the *New Review*. I got myself an office in Soho, a big
desk, two telephones, a small staff of willing helpers, a franking
machine. Much thought went into our letterhead design. And in
the pub downstairs I dreamed up savage business schemes,
thought big. 'A mailshot of so-and-so costs such-and-such.
Working on a two-and-a-half per cent return we'll effectively be
buying readers at so-much a head.' The fight was on, the life-raft
had set sail. The axe fell in 1979, and by then I had a long list of
why-nots: booksellers who wouldn't stock the magazine,
publishers who wouldn't advertise, readers who threw away the
mailshot without reading it, and so on. Then there was Edward
Heath, the three-day week, television, the Beatles. Overarchingly,
there was the general state of things, the culture, the shipwreck.
By the end of it, I was pretty glad to disembark.

For a year or two afterwards, however, I went around with a
long face. For some reason, and in spite of all the evidence, I
wanted people to believe that it hadn't been my fault.
Significantly, one of my darkest gripes was directed at the Arts

Council's Literature Panel. The Arts Council had been the *New Review*'s John Quinn. Like Quinn, it came up with the spondoolicks and for that it deserved, it still deserves, my thanks. Without its backing not even five issues of the magazine would have appeared, let alone the fifty that we eventually came through with. That was the Council, though. The Literature Panel was, as they say, a different kettle of fish. This powerful committee was staffed, alas, by writers.

And I mean alas. The truth is that when you give a bunch of writers any kind of money-muscle, they go slightly mad. I ought to know. And when you put them on committees that give money to other writers, they go madder still. I can hear their voices now: 'Mr Chairman, on a point of order, I feel it my duty to observe . . . ' And this would be some foppish, dreamy-faced poetaster fresh from a three-absinthe lunch. But nearly all of them behaved like this. Wild-eyed anarchic novelists would transmute into prim-lipped accountants. Tremulous lyric poets would rear up like tigers of the bottom line. Book-reviewers who, I knew, lived in daily terror of being rumbled by the Revenue were all at once furrow-browed custodians of *public funds*. Happily, I was only once called up to meet the Panel face to face. The event was like a cross between Star Chamber and our Prefects' Court at school. Afterwards I made a vow: from now on, I told the Council, I will deal only with career bureaucrats, with philistines. Show me an enemy of literature, and I will show him my accounts.

In a way, though, I was just as fake as those mad panellists. Like them I was pretending to be good with money, a safe pair of hands. And in November 1980, sitting in front of the Official Receiver, I was still faking. 'Our accumulated deficit was, let's say, thirty thousand pounds. Divide that by the fifty issues we produced and that's—what—about six hundred pounds per issue in arrears. Well, with our new typesetting machine, we might easily have taken in six hundred pounds worth of outwork, given half a chance. So we were not, as you seem to suggest, trading when non-viable. In my view, we were just about to turn the corner when those bastards pulled the plu . . . that is to say, when our creditors foreclosed.'

And so it went. The Receiver smiled me through it, but he

knew. He knew what I knew and what Pound knew. The whole thing had been 'wrong from the start', impossible, not on. For all Pound's craftiness, his skill at penetrating the corridors of wealth, for all his commonsensical acknowledgement of money's power, its self-regard, he was at heart a heretic, a money-apostate, a fake. And so was I.

Looking back on my first reading of Pound's letters, I can see now that it was not Pound the crusader who excited me so much as Pound the cultural outlaw. I liked the idea of being up against it, on the run and in the right. Certainly my best memories of those magazine years are of situations where the battle-lines were clearly marked, the hostilities explicit. When asked about the *New Review*, I am always more likely to boast about how I outwitted some bailiff than about this or that poem or short story. And my colleagues on the magazine feel much the same—especially those who are still waiting to be paid.

KEVIN JACKSON
TEN MONEY NOTES

1. Definitions

'Papa! what's money?'
Paul Dombey, *Dombey and Son*, Charles Dickens

Children can get away with asking what money is, but the question sounds silly when put by an adult. For most of us, the meaning of 'money' is obvious enough: it's the notes and coins in our pockets, the figures in our bank accounts, the stuff that we never have in sufficient quantity. Mr Dombey tells his young son that money is 'Guineas, shillings, half-pence,' and while those particular units of currency may be defunct today, the reply still sounds quite sensible.

It's not good enough for little Paul, though, who persists: 'Oh yes, I know what they are . . . I don't mean that, Papa. I mean what's money after all?' Paul's question is not practical; it echoes the ones asked by philosophers from Aristotle and Xenophon to Nietzsche and Georg Simmel, who would all have been dissatisfied with the textbook definition of money (more complete than Mr Dombey's, though not more imaginative) as a measure of value, a medium of exchange and a store of wealth.

Far from being self-evident, the nature of money is hard to pin down, and it is only because it features so prominently in our everyday lives that we tend to overlook its essential mystery. Something of that mystery remains in the hundreds of similes it has inspired. There are anatomical ones: in *Leviathan*, for instance, Hobbes likens money to blood, circulating around the commonwealth as blood courses around the body. Cicero saw money as the 'sinews of war', Edward Leigh (an early economist) as the sinews of government, and Sir William Petty (another such) as 'the Fat of the Body-politick': 'too much doth as often hinder its agility, as too little makes it sick.'

Money has been likened to oil (Hume), a cushion (Carl Sandburg), a bridge (Marshall McLuhan), a vehicle (Henry Ford, who knew about vehicles). More abstractly, it has been identified

Photo: Hulton Deutsch

Opposite: children play with bundles of notes during the period of hyperinflation in Germany, 1923

69

with liberty (Swift), happiness (Schopenhauer), ritual (Mary Douglas), art (Butler), thought (Spengler) and time (George Gissing, angrily inverting Ben Franklin's admonition that 'Time is Money'). Money has an extraordinary ability to stimulate metaphors, partly because it is itself—in the phrase of the American poet Dana Gioia—'the one true metaphor, the one commodity that can be translated into all else.' Marx, among other moralists, was both dazzled and horrified by the capacity of money to turn goods into services, services into goods, and itself into anything under the sun.

Despite money's protean nature, however, a lot of people persist in believing that it should stay much the same and are dismayed when it doesn't.

2. Change

> As a rule, there is nothing that offends us more than a
> new type of money.
>
> *The Pleasures of Ignorance,* Robert Lynd

When I was young, I bought my sweets and comics with the same coins Dickens handled. The guinea no longer existed except in the ledgers of the snootiest professions, and the farthing was all but extinct, but there was still a profusion of ha'pennies, thrup'ny bits, tanners, shillings, florins and half-crowns. I knew what it meant to sing a song of sixpence or to raise funds for charity at the rate of a bob a job; while, on the streets, to beg adults for 'a penny for the guy' before the Fifth of November was to quote a reasonable market rate.

For my generation, the transition from childhood to adolescence coincided with an uneasy national development: the decimalization of Britain's traditional currency. Instead of the colourful and weighty coins that I had learned to use (some bearing an inscription declaring that our monarch was still, somehow, the Empress of India), I now had to come to terms with such exotic specimens as a 'fifty-pence piece'.

Adults reserved a special dislike for the new penny. This coin, allegedly worth 2.4 times as much as its pre-decimal forebear, was pitifully slight, more like the humble farthing than the solid, honest copper (the English used to call both their specie and their trusted constabulary by the same robust nickname).

Such was the dislike for the *arriviste* coin that its jeering abbreviation has now become standard use: the new penny was called a p—or *pee*, a metamorphosis Anthony Burgess dismissed as a 'shameful liquidation'. The phrase hints at the deeper logic of the insult: Freud's suggestion that the unconscious identifies money with excrement—hence filthy lucre; hence the Bradford millionaire's maxim that 'where there's muck there's brass'; hence the expression, 'to spend a penny', long a coy euphemism for pissing.

I remember the game my grandfather played with me when I was five. He used to offer me a choice of pocket money: either six big pennies or a tiny sixpence. He got me every time: I always opted for the six heavy pennies. Grandparents, parents, aunts, uncles, the whole fraternity of grown-ups found this misapprehension hugely entertaining. It was bizarre, therefore, to witness only a few years later so many of the same adults playing another version of the old joke—this time with the puny, little pee. For a couple of years, decimalization made Britain into a nation of children.

In fact, Britain's pecuniary uneasiness had begun well before the advent of decimal coins. I was no different from any other child my age—economic developments were not one of my principal concerns—but there was one such development that was so shocking it registered in my mind alongside the things that really mattered (the Who's first single, for instance): the devaluation of the pound in 1967. The pound had always been big and strong—worth lots of Deutschmarks, French francs and American dollars. The pound, once worth as much as four dollars, was then worth three; then two dollars and forty cents, until, in 1985, it eventually reached near parity: in fact, in some

Photo: Popperfoto

Overleaf: ten-year-olds at Horsley Hill Junior School give their parents a lesson on how to use the new decimal coins, 1971.

London hotels, the dollar was worth more than the pound. Devaluation introduced doubts about the correspondence of words and things into the least philosophical minds. For all Harold Wilson's glib assurances at the time, everyone knew that the sterling in Britain's pocket was not what it had been. His 'perky mini-pound', as one tabloid christened it, trying to make industrial decline sound fun and sexy, was a whorish imposter.

3. A historical account

It may be objected that this connection between coins and treasure no longer holds for modern man; that paper money is in use everywhere; that the rich now keep their treasure in banks in an abstract and invisible form. But the importance of a gold reserve for a strong currency and the fact that there are still actual gold currencies to be found, prove that treasure has by no means entirely lost its old importance. The great majority of men, even in countries which are highly developed technically, are still paid for their work by the hour and, almost everywhere, the size of their wage still comes within the range imagined as covered by coins. Coins are still received as change for paper money, and the old feeling for them, the old attitude, is still familiar to everyone. Getting change is a daily part of the simplest and commonest processes of living, something which every child learns as early as possible.

Crowds and Power, Elias Canetti

The juvenile belief that a big coin must be worth more than a small one, and that many coins are worth more than a single one, can be described as a confusion between intellectual currency (the face value of money) and material currency (the value of the substance from which money is made). Once upon a time, it would have been impossible to make this mistake.

According to reputable accounts, the childhood years of

Picture: British Museum

MIDAS, Transmuting all into ~~GOLD~~ PAPER.

History of Midas,—— The great Midas having dedicated himself to Bacchus, obtained from that Deity, the Power of changing all he Touched.—
Apollo fixed Asses Ears upon his head, for his Ignorance.— & although he tried to hide his disgrace with a Regal Cap, yet the very Sedges which grew
from the Mud of the Pactolus, whisperd out his Infamy, whenever they were agitated by the Wind from the opposite Shore.— Vide Ovids Metamorphoses.

money itself—western money, anyway—were spent in ancient Greece. Lydia was the first state to mint coins, in about the eighth century BC, and for a time Lydia's intellectual currency and its material currency were one. The earliest Lydian coins were made of an alloy known as electrum, and their value was taken to be identical to their weight. In this respect, as some theologians have described it, money was once like the language of Adam before the Fall: there was no separation between word and thing.

But it was also the Greeks—or, at least their rulers—who realized that a coin's worth could be changed, not by adding to or subtracting from its material weight, but by stamping words and pictures on its front and back and declaring its new value. Money fell from grace, and has been falling ever since, though news of the Fall circulated more quickly in some places than in others.

Outside the West, you can still find a currency that derives its value from its utility or beauty: the edible cow, for instance, or the decorative cowrie shell. And it has often been the case that a nation colonizing a new frontier resorts to the type of cash you can consume: Roman centurions stationed far from the Imperial mints were paid in salt (hence the word 'salary'), and the first North American settlers traded in tobacco when coins were in short supply

Curiously, it took a very long time for the West to understand that you could make money from something as flimsy as paper. When Marco Polo told Europe that the Grand Khan in China issued paper money, he was accused of lying. It wasn't until the Romantic period that paper money began to infiltrate western economies, and, even then, it was strongly resisted. Workers refused to take notes for their wages, and shopkeepers would not exchange them for goods.

Today, when the gap between intellectual currency and material currency is wider than ever, such outrage seems quaint. It would be hard to find tribes so remote from the workings of the global economy that they would refuse a dollar bill, and no one seems to mind that most of the world's money now takes the form of intangible units of information that computers shuffle from state to state. (As Marc Shell has pointed out in *Money, Language and Thought*, money began its career as electrum and had ended as electricity: 'The matter of electric money does not matter.')

But this is not to say that our understanding of the workings of money is now any more mature or rational. After all, the recognition that money is only of relative, social value has been common since Aristotle, who pointed out that the Greek word for 'money' was derived from the Greek word for 'law': money works because all of us tacitly consent that it should; outside society, it makes no sense at all. At any rate, that's the rational view; but there is a famously revealing moment in *Robinson Crusoe* which shows how feeble the rational view can be.

Crusoe, raiding his wrecked ship for food, drink and tools, comes across a locker full of coins. He is moved to rhetoric worthy of any pulpit:

> 'O drug!' said I aloud, 'what art thou good for? Thou art not worth to me . . . One of these knives is worth all this heap. I have no manner of use for thee; even remain where thou art, and go to the bottom as a creature whose life is not worth saving.'

Sensible fellow. But then Defoe delivers the punchline: 'However, upon second thoughts, I decided to take it away.' Just in case.

4. Bubbles and crashes

> But there's no doubt but money is to the fore now. It is the romance, the poetry of our age. It's the thing that chiefly strikes the imagination. The Englishmen who come here are more curious about the great new millionaires than about anyone else, and they respect them more. It's all very well. I don't complain of it.
>
> *The Rise of Silas Lapham*, William Dean Howells

It is hardest to be philosophical about money when everyone around you is obsessed by it. Even genius is not immune to collective greed. Sir Isaac Newton—who besides his work in physics, alchemy and Biblical commentary was also Master of the Royal Mint—was briefly possessed by the spirit of Gordon Gekko. In 1720, shortly before the end of that episode of speculative mania known as the South Sea Bubble, Newton decided that the shares he had bought had appreciated quite sufficiently. He sold them. But the market continued its steep climb, and Newton succumbed to greed. He bought again, at an inflated price. Then the Bubble burst. According to legend, Newton's rueful judgement on the whole episode was that he could predict the movements of celestial bodies but not the follies of men.

One thing you *can* predict about such bubbles is that they will always recur, even though everyone knows that every bubble eventually bursts. At about the same time as the South Sea episode, France was going through a financial lunacy of its own, the so-called Mississippi Bubble. Stocks in a fanciful scheme for developing the Louisiana wilderness rose so rapidly that, in 1719, an investment of a few thousand livres yielded millions in a matter of weeks. (This was the year in which the word *millionaire* was born.) The Bubble ended in July 1720, with a crowd storming the Banque Royale in Paris, demanding hard money in return for their securities; fifteen people were crushed to death. Washington Irving wrote a vivid history of the event, and his phrase for that period just before the inevitable crash has an agreeable irony: 'A Time of Unexampled Prosperity.'

You did not need much wit to notice that the prosperity of the 1980s really was unexampled. Electric money flowed round the planet in unprecedented quantities; fortunes were made with stupefying rapidity. And even though capitalism took some nasty stumbles, such as Black Monday and the savings-and-loans fiasco, it still emerged enough of a winner by the end of the decade to gloat over the fall of its biggest rival, communism. No one was untouched by the convulsions of the market. Those outside the feeding frenzy might have been appalled, might, in fact, have been shocked into an awareness of the raw, amoral power of lucre for the very first time; but they could not deny that money was more powerful—and, therefore, more seductive—than ever before.

'Could this delusion always last, the life of the merchant would indeed be a golden dream; but it is as short as it is brilliant,' Washington Irving wrote. The golden dreamers of the eighties woke up to global recession. Britain has fudged and panicked its way out of the Exchange Rate Mechanism, and Eastern Europe has found that a capitalist omelette, like the old communist kind, also requires the breaking of eggs.

But if money doesn't look quite so dazzling now as it did in the years leading up to the crash of 1987, it is hard to point to any promising new contenders. If only by default, money is still what Heine called it: the God of this world.

5. Interest

All money, properly so called, is an acknowledgement of debt.

Unto this Last, John Ruskin

Lending is such a serious matter that it's hard to exaggerate its importance. Even so, the word 'usury' has a fusty smell for us. It belongs to an epoch in which the pious believed that it was one of the blackest of crimes, forbidden by scripture and by Aristotle (the Koran is equally harsh). To lend at interest was to trade blasphemously in time, which belonged only to God. To gather money without working for it was to shirk Adam's penance for original sin, the earning of bread by the sweat of his brow. To take the profits made possible by other men's labour was open theft.

Many reputable scholars have written studies of usury and its role in the history of anti-Semitism, but only one modernist writer has looked on it with a loathing of medieval intensity and made a campaign against it central to his life's work: Ezra Pound.

Though Pound may have been doomed to his money obsession by his family name and his childhood experiences (his father worked as an assayer at the United States Mint), he showed little interest in the subject until he came to London shortly before the First World War. Bracingly immodest, he wanted to bring about a twentieth-century renaissance in the arts, but saw that the most promising talents of his generation—Eliot, Joyce, the sculptor Gaudier-Brzeska—were too busy chasing pennies to achieve their best work.

He concluded that great artists required great patrons and set about recruiting suitable candidates. At the same time, the war (in which Gaudier-Brzeska died) sent Pound's mind off hunting along other lines: who profited by such a slaughter? The shape of history began to look different to him. Before long, he was claiming that he could tell the degree of usury that prevailed in any given period by looking at its paintings. *Usura* produced thick lines, blurring, fug. Moreover, behind the First World War, he perceived a less obvious conflict: a struggle across the ages between the forces of usury and the forces of light.

Pound needed heroes. He made one eccentric choice—Major Douglas, the proponent of an economic doctrine known as Social Credit—and one disastrous choice: Benito Mussolini. The poet's vocal enthusiasm for the Duce eventually put him in a cage at a US Army detention centre in Pisa and then, after he had been declared unfit to stand trial for treason, in a mental hospital in Washington. In his sad old age, the poet fell into almost total, penitent silence, and put it on the record that his rage against usury and the Jews had been a terrible mistake. The true enemy was avarice.

Pound's life reads like a modern morality tale, although the precise nature of the moral remains unclear. (The simplest reading is that exceptional literary talent will not keep you from making pernicious judgements.) Certain parts of the *Cantos* are repellent: it is charitable to think him mad, rather than evil when he wrote them. But if you are horrified by accounts of Third World debts, or think of the effects of market forces on art, or if you are being crushed by iniquitous rates of interest, then Pound's early writings may seem a lot more sympathetic.

6. Filthy lucre

No thing in use by man, for power of ill,
Can equal money. This lays cities low,
This drives men forth from quiet dwelling place,
This warps and changes minds of worthiest stamp,
To turn to deeds of baseness, teaching men
All shifts of cunning, and to know the guilt
Of every impious deed.

Antigone, Sophocles

Money is the root of all evil: so says the proverb, so say the wise men across the centuries. Money drives humankind to fraud, forgery, theft and murder. It bribes judges, corrupts the young, makes sons crave the death of their fathers and keeps the wicked out of prison. It makes artists debase their talent, drives out excellence and enshrines the vulgar and fake. It undermines every form of human decency.

Railing against the tyranny of Mammon is an ancient refrain and has not always been quite as marginal as it was in the eighties. When a socialist historian such as R. H. Tawney looked at the middle ages, in *Religion and the Rise of Capitalism*, he discovered a social order which, whatever its other ills, was obliged to take what preachers said into account, and the preachers were certain that this new rising class of money men were a terrible threat. As a result, the middle ages ordered some matters better than we order ours—at least according to Tawney. Such practices as upholding the 'Just Price', prohibiting excessive interest rates, recognizing that man is a divine creature before he is a commercial unit were all healthier, Tawney felt, than the ruthless calculations of the market. No wonder the rise of *homo economicus* seemed like a visitation from Lucifer.

Though recent centuries have cared more for their profits than their prophets, there have been one or two occasions when moralists have found an attentive audience. Victorian sages such as Thomas Carlyle, John Ruskin and William Morris were the heirs of the medieval theologians, and their words had a palpable influence.

Nowadays Ruskin is not much read outside courses on Victorian literature, but *Unto this Last* was the *Little Red Book* of its day and inspired not only the first generation of Labour politicians but also Mahatma Gandhi.

Were the sages and theologians mistaken in thinking money an abomination? Did they make an elementary confusion between money itself, which is a tool as neutral as fire, and the lusts it engenders? After all, that old proverb is a misquotation. The book of Timothy identifies the root of evil not as money, but as *cupiditas*, the love of money. To hate money for providing the temptation to crime is like hating metal because guns and bullets are made from it.

7. Credits

> You tell me that money cannot buy the things most precious. Your commonplace proves that you have never known the lack of it. When I think of all the sorrow and the barrenness that has been wrought in my life by want of a few more pounds per annum than I was able to earn, I stand aghast at money's significance . . . I think it would scarce be an exaggeration to say that there is no moral good which has not to be paid for in coin of the realm.
>
> *The Private Papers of Henry Ryecroft*, George Gissing

Of course, money is wonderful, and a whiff of fake piety, not to say hypocrisy, hangs around the texts that say otherwise. As he was well aware, Ruskin's own diatribes on the subject were made possible by his private income (which does not discredit them), and he enjoyed to the full all the good things that money can buy, from paintings to travel. Hardly anyone is sufficiently ascetic to resist the delight of a sudden windfall, and most people realize that the idea of wealth bringing misery is a myth, propagated to cheer up the poor.

Money builds cities and hospitals and universities, saves

lives, feeds the hungry, clothes and houses the cold, stimulates science, supports the arts, creates beauty and order. In short, it is the basis for civilization, as Edward Gibbon wrote in his history of the Roman Empire: 'Money . . . is the most universal incitement, iron the most powerful instrument, of human industry; and it is very difficult to conceive by what means a people, neither actuated by the one nor seconded by the other, could emerge from the grossest barbarism.'

Keynes went further and proposed that the lack of major technological change between the dawn of human history and the early eighteenth century was due to the failure of capital to accumulate. The modern world was born, he asserted, out of the rising European prices and profits that resulted from importing gold and silver from the New World. Without inflation and compound interest, there would have been no Industrial Revolution.

Whether or not such speculations are well-founded, it is clear that the benefits of money are immense. Some of the exuberance of the 1980s was due to this fact: greed may never be good, but money often is. Most of us are confused by this distinction, and our attitudes towards money tend to be deeply contradictory. It is prudent and honourable to work hard for money; it is venal to pursue money for its own sake. If we work for hire, we are hacks; if we work for nothing, we are chumps. Fond of money ourselves, we sentimentalize the people who are meant to spurn it, and are shocked when they prove to be every bit as sensible as we are.

8. Coining phrases

When I expressed an earnest wish for his remarks on Italy, [Dr Johnson] said, 'I do not see that I could make a book upon Italy; yet I should be glad to get two hundred pounds, or five hundred pounds, by such a work.' This shewed both that a journal of his Tour upon the Continent was not wholly out of his contemplation, and that he uniformly adhered to that strange opinion, which his indolent disposition made him utter: 'No man but a blockhead ever wrote, except for money.'

The Life of Samuel Johnson, James Boswell

Idealistic readers, such as Boswell here, may be disillusioned by the fact that authors should want to be paid well, believing literature should have nothing to do with money. But literature, as Boswell would also have known, has always been a trade as well as a calling: writers, like any other professional, deserve to be paid for their products. Johnson, who wrote at a time when authors were turning away from the fickle patronage of noblemen to the fickle patronage of the book-buying public, was keenly aware of what independence costs.

In fact, for many writers cash itself provides their most fascinating subject-matter: where would the nineteenth-century novel be without money? There are, too, some deeper affinities between literature and money: both, after all, are systems for representing reality. From a disinterested perspective, what is the difference between a wad of banknotes and the manuscript of a book? Both are finally nothing more than stacks of paper sheets that derive their value from the markings made across them.

And even if this were not so, a writer who shunned all mention of money would be accepting a self-limitation every bit as perverse as Georges Perec's resolution to eschew the letter *E* in writing his novel *La Disparition*. A writer's task is to describe, interpret and remake the world; and money—so Shaw provocatively declared—is the most important thing in the world.

9. Values

In Germany, the want of worldly goods is very amiably excused, and with us genius may suffer and hunger without being despised. In England men are less tolerant; a man's merit is there measured by his income, and 'How much is he worth?' means literally, either, 'How much money has he?' or 'What are his merits?' I myself once heard a burly Englishman seriously ask a Franciscan monk how much he made annually by going about barefoot with a rope round his body?

Lutetia, Heinrich Heine

Can the value of something really be the same as its market price? The obvious answer is no, and we are uncomfortable when money is used as a supreme arbiter—so much so that there is a whole school of black jokes on the theme. In Martin Amis's novel *Money*, a yobbish father presents his son with an itemized bill for his upbringing. And Woody Allen used to have a gag in his stand-up routine in which he would display his watch to the audience and tearfully explain that the timepiece had enormous value to him because it had belonged to his grandfather. When the old man was breathing his last, he summoned his grandson to the bedside, took off the watch and, after a bit of bargaining, sold it to young Woody.

Even so, it is impossible for market valuations not to colour other types of value. Robert Hughes has written that no aesthetic arguments, theories, fashions or fads of the past decades have affected our sense of painting and sculpture nearly so fundamentally as the investment capital that has moved into the art market. Every famous painting, not just Andy Warhol's sequence of dollar bills, now represents a vast pile of cash. And however fulsome the lip-service a society may pay to the professions which do not directly produce wealth—teaching, nursing, fighting fires—the salaries of those engaged in these jobs reveal what the society really considers valuable.

It takes a fierce independence to feel that your personal worth has nothing whatsoever to do with the price you can command in the marketplace. (Hence the psychological miseries of unemployment or low-paid work, often more painful than their practical woes.) It takes a still more resolute soul to feel confident of a solid identity in times when the circulating medium is in a state of flux.

During periods of economic stability, it is easy to believe that the value of money is firm and eternal. But if a moderate measure of inflation, shaking this faith, can help make people more reflective, hyperinflation is not so ennobling. One of the most telling arguments of Canetti's *Crowds and Power* is that the loss of meaning that befell Germany's currency in the 1920s also made individual lives seem worthless—especially if those lives were Jewish. Inflation led to barbarism. When money breaks down, morality breaks down too.

10. Penniless Utopias

> The love of money as a possession—as distinguished from the love of money as a means to the enjoyments and realities of life—will be recognized for what it is, a somewhat disgusting morbidity, one of those semi-criminal, semi-pathological propensities which one hands over with a shudder to the specialists in mental disease.
>
> 'Economic Possibilities for our Grandchildren,'
> J. M. Keynes

When visionaries muse on the subject of money, they imagine a perfect world that has no money in it. Some of these Utopian schemes have actually been put into practice. According to Plutarch, Lycurgus scrapped Sparta's existing money and replaced it with huge, unwieldy blocks of iron of negligible value. 'With the diffusion of this substitute money, at once a number of vices were banished from Sparta; for who would rob another of such a coin? Who would unjustly detain or take by force, or accept as a bribe, a thing that was not easy to hide, nor a credit to have, nor any use to cut to pieces?' And though communist states have been reluctant to get rid of money altogether, Spanish anarchists tried to do so in Andalusia and Catalonia during the 1930s, as did Pol Pot in Cambodia.

Most monetary Utopias, though, remain on paper: Sir Thomas More's influential republic, where the chamber pots are made of gold; Campanella's City of the Sun; Robert Owen's New Moral World; the transfigured England of William Morris's

News from Nowhere; the absolutely benign welfare state of Edward Bellamy's *Looking Backward* (the first novel to envisage the use of credit cards).

The most common metaphor these visionaries use is one of growing up: a truly adult social order, they suggest, would have no need of stores of wealth, measures of value, media of exchange. This may seem persuasive, especially if you have just lived through some monetary catastrophe such as a crash or an inflation. But is it not a little perverse to believe that you attain maturity by shedding cash? After all it is adults, not children, who know and care about money, as well as every other kind of symbolic acquisition. Freud once suggested that money can't buy happiness because happiness (or adult pleasure, at least) results only from

Above: Berlin, 1923. Hyperinflation meant that workers had to collect their pay-packets in laundry baskets.

gratifying infantile desires: and infants don't want money.

Craving for a society without money is, in fact, regressive. It looks back not simply to childhood but to infancy, when coins were just hazardous playthings and we didn't have the words to ask what money was. Monetary Utopians would like to be even more innocent than little Paul Dombey.

A healthy corrective to such enthusiastic schemes comes, as so often, from Samuel Johnson:

> To mend the world by banishing money is an old contrivance of those who did not consider that the quarrels and mischiefs which arise from money must, if money were to cease, arise immediately from riches themselves; and could never be at an end till every man was contented with his own share of the goods of life.

Of all the alleged evils that stand between us and Utopia, the least baleful is money.

Opposite: banknotes abandoned in the courtyard of the National Bank of Cambodia after Pol Pot suppressed all money.

GRANTA

JAMES BUCHAN
THE PSYCHOLOGY OF MONEY

A s a child and teenager, I had little to do with money. I was educated on scholarships and state hand-outs and the kindness of strange adults, and this money passed over my head. I started thinking seriously about money only in 1978, in the city of Jeddah on the Red Sea.

I had come to Jeddah to delay my induction into the money society at home, to postpone the passage into adulthood.

I had got a job working at a newspaper I'll call the *Saudi News*. It was in a plywood building at the end of the airport runway. The newspaper, the building and the airport have all since vanished, for they were embarrassing physical reminders of an earlier age in Saudi history, the years before 1973, before money. The quadruple rise in the price of crude oil at the end of that year had detonated the world's trading system, and money was streaming into Saudi Arabia as nowhere and never before, trailing its usual baggage of power and influence. The burden of history had passed to a few pale, fat men gliding like phantoms at noon into their Lincolns. The Muslim civilizations of Egypt and India, with their ancient architecture and worldly cultures, had become worthless; Europeans and Americans waited for days in the ante-rooms of dozing assistant deputy under-secretaries of state; the British, who had once set up and knocked down these princelings, wheedled and bribed with the best of them.

For two years, every day of the week except Thursday, I left home at three in the afternoon and crossed the silent, blazing city to this ramshackle hut. I worked till three in the morning. As I walked home, there might be a fugitive breath of wind, though it was never cool. Sometimes I found myself in fabulous suburbs which had not existed the week before, raised like volcanic islands, an eruption of money. Stretched out on my sodden bed, as the air-conditioners began to beat, beat, beat in unison, I thought that whatever I'd expected of life, it wasn't this. An hour or two later, the *Saudi News* was delivered and confirmed my existence, yet with inexplicable injuries: here a caption dropped, there King Khaled cropped to his nostrils, a story unravelled like an old sleeve to fill an aching void of white on an inside page.

The room I worked in had two windows blocked by air-conditioners, four steel desks, four burst chairs and four manual

Photo: G. Rancinan (Sygma)

typewriters; a telephone with one outside line, a glutinous carpet and a strip of fluorescent light. Each Wednesday night, the last of the lunar month, I sensed the room begin to shake and roar; the accountant glided in with his briefcase and flip-flops; a blizzard of Arabic greeting; and then the haul of envelopes from the briefcase, like fish pulled in on a hand-line. Sheathed in air-conditioned sweat, I would sign for ten thousand Saudi Arabian riyals in bills—bundles of them, held by twine, the price of a month's labour, boredom and misery.

This moment was supposed to appear—and perhaps did appear to some of my friends in the room—as a moment of unity that abolished our identities as British or Yemeni or Indian or Egyptian, and confirmed us as men who labour and are paid. The banknotes, with portraits of King Abdul Aziz bin Saud (who never had any money until Standard Oil of California gave him thirty-five thousand gold sovereigns in 1933) or King Faisal (who was murdered), were our common consolation for the nights of work and days without sleep, the indifference of our hosts, the misery of our women if we had them and of our solitude if we hadn't. And for this treadmill of heat.

But within the consolation of money was an exasperation. These banknotes inflamed our particular national humiliations and would have been intolerable but for another secret they bore: they were the means of escape. Not escape in the sense they could buy an airplane ticket to Sanaa or Djibouti, for we were a class of indentured servants and could not leave the country without a visa from the Foreign Office which must also be endorsed by the proprietor of the newspaper, but in the sense that they promised us an existence away from this hell-hole: a corner shop one day in Murree or Dindigul, or a rental flat in Helwan, or a father's brother's daughter just turning sixteen. For a moment, these dreams of liberty vibrated in the roaring plywood room.

The moment dissipated. My friends picked up their money, gripping the twine between the middle and index finger of the right hand, flicked it over and with the thumb counted the notes fanned by the counterforce of the flick. This action, both familiar and deft, occupied them for half a minute, but I left my money uncounted. I was indifferent to its sum, not just because a missing hundred-riyal note really made no difference in a 10,000-riyal bundle, but also because I sensed that indifference, the vice and virtue of the British, was my chief protection in this jail and alone linked me to our masters, who themselves never really believed in the prosperity that fell on them in the space of a few days in October 1973, and could quite happily have returned to herding and growing dates and trading bullion and fleecing pilgrims. (In fact, the Saudis did squander their fortune, first in equipping the Iraqi armed forces and then, in 1991, in paying British and United States mercenaries to destroy them.)

What need did I have of money? There was nothing I wanted to buy in the *suq*, except a camera with a long lens to photograph baboons (which I subsequently broke over somebody's head and didn't replace) and whisky, which came in the holds of C-130 aircraft and cost 250 riyals a bottle (about a hundred pounds today). I had no interest in what people now call positional goods, for where were my witnesses, my publicists? Not in this demoralized Babel or among my generation in Britain, which was absorbed in a society that was manifestly on its last legs: the future, in the shape of Margaret Thatcher's handbag, was at that moment struggling to take shape. I didn't care to provide for my old age, for I didn't think I'd have one. Anyway, I couldn't put out the money at interest, for interest was *haram*, anathema, and the banks paid their depositors just half a per cent of commission (while they lent their money abroad at eight per cent and earned fabulous profits and no doubt a fair stay in hell). I could not own real estate, for this was denied to foreigners. I could not put the money at risk, for there was no stock market.

I read Adam Smith for the first time that year. I knew that of the three great, original and constituent orders of society he identified, I belonged not with the landowner or capitalist, but the labourer. I received labourer's wages, the real value of which arose not in the money I received but—Smith again—in what could be got with it, and that was nothing. I was a slave.

A man of twenty-three should occupy his thoughts with young women. If they are abstracted from him, if they are so alien that he forgets even their anatomy, his mind has empty places which must be colonized. Of the young women I'd abandoned, I had few mementoes: a diamond bracelet that spelt the name of a famous mare, with its hasp broken—I was anxious to return it and did—and the odd letter which might once have contained some crystalline cocaine; if so, it had since been dissolved into the paper by the humidity and was therefore useless for sensation or commerce or patronage or any purpose except that of getting me executed. After a while, these women seemed to me inexplicable, as if of a different element, of water or sky.

In my inferno of solitude, I thought there must be some reason why I was doing what I was doing. For a while, I told myself I was learning a trade. But going into the press at three in the morning, crushing a ball of paper to throw at the printer in his Madras kilt, I sensed that I was the last man in the world to learn hot-metal typesetting. No doubt I was also learning Arabic, a difficult language, but in reality, I was forgetting even the moderate amount I knew.

There were occasions that year when I felt a sort of relief, most often in the desert at night or in the deep sea. On the escarpment behind the town, while trucks grunted round the hairpins on the road up to Taif, I gaped at the squabbling baboons as the sun turned to ghee in the west; as it dissolved in the sea, the animals would fall silent and sit, motionless, looking westward, as if they too were inclined to melancholy. Or descending into deep water, scuba diving, I felt a calm come over me. Once, coming up, at the limit of my compressed air, I passed into a band of turbid water and realized there must be a sandstorm overhead. I rose into hot hail and razor sand, no sun or tide to indicate the shore. I had a choice: to float on my tanks until some hand scooped me up as one might a dead locust off a swimming-pool—a very unattractive form of extinction—or to cast the tanks adrift and go down, by the weight of my legs and belt, resurfacing again and again, each foot of depth an agony of nitrogen and panic, until the reef appeared in the gloom and showed the way back to shore.

My purpose was not simply to die, it seemed, and it was not to learn a trade, or Arabic or experience the dignity of labour. My real purpose must have been money. What was this thing, this rectangle of watermarked paper, engraved by De La Rue in London but now stinking from some Sudanese labourer's armpit, worthless in itself, but available for hoarding or commerce by consent (although *badu* taxi-drivers would sometimes reject a clean note, merely because it felt obscurely wrong to them)? What was this thing, stronger than love of liberty or women, self-respect and despair; or rather that drew into itself a portion of all these sentiments? It seemed to me that since I wasn't going to die, or not for a while, I should do something with the interval, and what better than to study this thing, make it my life, wrestle with it as Jacob with the angel?

I was not interested in the operation of money in society or the creation of social wealth. The science we now call economics seemed to me, from a study of the Saudi political economy— admittedly primitive—modest in its aims. In reality, economics has fallen prey to the very social mechanisms it attempts to describe and authorize; the various theories merely confirm or deny the privileges or fantasies of social classes. Even Keynes, whom I was reading, seemed riven by a simultaneous avarice and contempt for money, and parts of the *General Theory* just didn't make sense. I stuck with Aristotle, since for him economics was a matter of the private or household sphere (what we call economics he called politics); his Christian and Muslim commentators in the middle ages; and the clerical theorists of inflation in sixteenth-century Spain. I wanted to know how people felt about money.

I recognized at this early stage that there were pathological aspects to my enquiry, that my interest in money arose from disordered tracts of my biography, and that money represented for me something in my early life that did not bear thinking about, to do with margarine and funerals and dismantled rooms: in short, the loss of childhood. It occurred to me that, in occupying myself with money, I might restore that disordered period without the bother and expense of psychoanalysis; anyway, I was not sure that Freud, in his self-analysis, devoted sufficient time to money, or that the psychoanalytic fee, that pillar of Freudian analysis, was quite so clinically self-evident as the founder made out.

James Buchan

In 1980, I picked fights with several influential men and was politely shown the way to the airport. I converted my bundles of riyals into sterling: they made, I guess, about thirty thousand pounds, about seventy-five thousand today. Because I regarded money with suspicion, I changed it into property of one type or another, which accorded with the spirit of an inflationary age. The money was, in its time, a mortgaged house in Lavender Hill, a glacially slow racehorse, stock in the Dresdner Bank, an excessive number of eighteenth-century engravings of St Petersburg, an apartment in lower Manhattan, stock in supermarket corporations. At each transition, it shed chips to stockbrokers, picture dealers, realtors, the Inland Revenue, the Customs and Excise, the IRS and the Federal Taxation Office, but always reassembled itself into more money than at its previous dissolution. I travelled the world at this period and assembled an obsessive collection of banknotes which I stored in the drawer of an old desk my mother had left me in her will: a highly symptomatic action, I recognize. There were Yemeni and Iranian riyals, Kuwaiti and Iraqi dinars, West and East German marks, United States and Fijian and Maria Theresa dollars, zlotys, roubles, rupees, shekels, Ecuadorean sucres, Mexican and Chilean pesos, French and Swiss francs, British, Turkish and Egyptian pounds. I also had a mineral from Antarctica, collected from an outcrop at eighty degrees south of latitude, to commemorate a barter economy, where exchange and value subsisted in cigarettes, *pisco*, aviation spirit and the blessed warmth of Red Army-issue felt boots.

This was not a miser's collection; with a few exceptions, the banknotes became useless as a hoard or medium of exchange. I experimented once with a high Turkish bill, ten years old, which I presented at Istanbul airport in the belief it might still buy a packet of cigarettes. It couldn't buy Chiclets. I kept the notes because I liked to sense their value evaporating, their money-ness seeping into the old satinwood until they were just coloured paper. I thought that one day I'd be picked up in the middle of Threadneedle Street, gabbling fragments of old Greek and incorrect balance-sheet ratios, and be led off to some secure location where there is no money.

At about this time, a further change came over my life. The

money from Jeddah began to breed, convulsively. While I slept, or was drunk, or made love, or smoked a Benson on the porch, my money worked and, as far as I could tell, for greater reward than I did. I felt a regret: the lightness which comes with empty pockets, the airy, tremulous sense of self which had been mine throughout my teens, the alienation from even the fabric of commercial society, its street corners and bullying office blocks and lighted shops, was now lost to me, possibly for ever. I felt obscurely disabled. It was as if the subject of my enquiry, while relieving me of labour and care, were also mocking me.

In analysing this new situation, I thought perhaps there was some quality about my labour from 1978 to 1980, some particular virtue that gave it uncommon power in commanding the labour of others. I once accosted a man in the South Seas who was planting some taro root; he told me that this action, which took up a full twenty minutes of a rainy morning, was enough to keep his family in food and grog and cash for a year. No doubt at the depths of every *rentier*'s existence, from duke to retiree, there is the faint shadow cast by some dead labour, but it is lost in the glitter of possession and present income.

This onset of prosperity did have one benign psychological effect. In my childhood, the possessor of money might have been virtuous or wicked, but he or she wore an authority that was somehow inherent in money riches. Even money's servants, like the bank manager in his panelled office, were figures of power, wisdom and restraint. Since my money had come to me without much by way of ability or virtue, and from only a couple of years' labour, these authorities were revealed as shams, and I was free to pursue my enquiry without their psychological invigilation.

In this, I was fortunate. The disesteem of money, symbolized by inflation, existed alongside a new and exaggerated esteem for money. In Britain, Germany, the states of central Europe, Russia, Latin America—indeed, everywhere I went, but particularly in Britain—money was quickly displacing all other psychological goals. Duty, religion, public service, liberty, equality, justice or aristocracy, the cultural flesh that clothed the bones of money for those that possessed it, all became suspect: only money, it seemed, was to be trusted. In Britain, at least, this undoubtedly had to do with the frustrations of those dynamic social groups—young people, immigrants, women—who had had it up to here with the senile prattle of a society they thought ripe for the boneyard. In Russia and Eastern Europe, money took on the character of emancipation and modernity more comprehensively than even the early paper money of the United States or the first issues of *assignats* in revolutionary Paris: it was Dostoevsky, after all, who described money as 'coined liberty', and in the *Manifesto of the Communist Party* of 1848, Marx and Engels showed a healthy respect for capitalism:

> The bourgeoisie, by the rapid improvement of all instruments of production, by the immensely facilitated means of communication, draws all, even the most barbarian, nations into civilization. The cheap prices of its commodities are the heavy artillery with which it batters down all Chinese walls, with which it forces the barbarians' intensely obstinate hatred of foreigners to capitulate.

Only money could measure success or failure, happiness or misery. Only money could reward or punish. States and governments must just stand back, and money—which contains all knowledge and reconciles all clashes of human will—would see us right. Money was good.

I had learned by then that money is our greatest invention, has done more to make our civilization even than letters—for these must be translated, whereas money is the language that every human being speaks and understands. Money has made easy the movements of people and ideas, given us world wars and monuments of architecture, transformed our notions of luxury or want. As a means, I saw that money was almost absolute: it could realize every fantasy of creation or murder. It could even give life, in the sense that hundreds of millions of people would not be alive today—could not be fed—but for the pattern of world trade made possible by money. And at this moment of extreme abstraction, it was transforming once again: into an absolute end. Money was valued not for its power to fulfil wishes: rather it was the goal of all wishes. Money was enthroned as the god of our times.

I was in New York on the morning of 19 October 1987 and felt the foundation of this new religion shake. That morning, I concluded that a failure of money in two of its aspects—measure of value and medium of exchange—was possible, ever more so as money increased in abstraction, losing even the gossamer physicality of banknotes and becoming a mere impulse in an electronic ledger. In London and New York, I met people who invested fortunes in financial enterprises they simply could not define or explain. No doubt quite soon, a bank would discover it had lost its capital in these obscure speculations; other banks would fall in sympathy; there would be a depression in trade; trade wars; killing wars.

It was also clear to me that the contradictory attitudes to money at this time—its esteem and disesteem—could not last indefinitely and must be resolved, and that did indeed happen. In May 1990, a picture evidently painted by Van Gogh sold in New York for eighty-two-and-a-half million dollars: that is, an oil portrait of one Dr Gachet sold for eighty-two-and-a-half million engraved portraits of George Washington. Everybody, except perhaps the directors of Christie's, decided this was excessive, and the price of objects as expressed in money fell; the price of money, as expressed in objects or in the rate of interest, rose. The esteem of money was complete.

Back in London, on a table at a junk fair in Hampstead, among fake Bohemian glass and ratty trinkets, I saw a set of currency notes in a Cellophane wrapper. Behind the table was a small old woman. She seemed fragile, cunning, old-fashioned, cossetted, like a painted Easter egg in cotton wool. I sensed she must have been hard-used at one time, and had not lived much or changed her habits since then. I looked at the glass and trinkets and then, in an off-hand way, at the notes.

'How much are these?'

She looked at me. She was trying to establish their value in British money, which was not easy for her, because they had no value to her and, because she did not know of my obsession, she did not know their value to me. She could not judge my willingness to buy, only my ability, and for that she must look to my appearance, which was not encouraging: I was wearing jeans and flip-flops and had not shaved. I had abandoned financial speculation, and even spending money, except in a new addiction to tobacco: the gold of the packet soothed and excited me more than ever the metal.

'It'll have to be twenty-five pounds. They're . . . '

I knew what they were. At that moment, my thoughts, though not necessarily in this order, were: how deep are the ironies of my enquiry that for these currency notes, which never ever bought anything, I am about to exchange something that will buy this lady heat or light or *Kaffee und Kuchen*; and that I am now reversing the famous law that holds that bad money drives out good. The money in its wrapper on the table was not just bad, it was the worst ever minted. I picked up the notes and put them down again. The topmost was biscuit-coloured, watermarked, in good condition. Its face value was a hundred crowns. It was dated 1 January 1943 in Austrian German and signed by a Jakob Edelstein. Its reverse showed the sum and a warning in High German which read, ANY PERSON COUNTERFEITING OR COPYING THESE BILLS OR HANDLING FORGED BILLS WILL BE SEVERELY PUNISHED. In a roundel was a nice portrait of Moses carrying the Ten Commandments.

I paid twenty pounds.

These notes, which were signed by the Chief Elder of the Council of Jews in the concentration camp of Theresienstadt in Bohemia and issued as wages or dole, barely circulated and were used chiefly as counters in card games. Jakob Edelstein was murdered at Birkenau on 20 July 1944. The notes stood in the same relation to reality as the postcards which deported prisoners sent from Upper Silesia: *The journey was exhausting but without incident. Omi sends love.* The fraud and consolation inherent in all money becomes, in these *Ghettokronen*, pure deceit, pure fantasy. People believed in them, as we all believe in money, because without it we cannot live in the world. As Byron kept a skull upon his desk, so I keep these notes in their Cellophane wrapper so that I do not forget the people of Theresienstadt and my eventual pauper's grave.

GRANTA

JONATHAN RABAN
BAD LAND

Breasting the regular swells of land, on a red dirt road as true as a line of longitude, the car was like a boat at sea. The ocean was hardly more solitary than this empty country, where in forty miles or so I hadn't seen another vehicle. A warm westerly blew over the prairie, making waves, and when I wound down the window I heard it growl in the dry grass like surf. For gulls, there were killdeer plovers, crying out their name as they wheeled and skidded on the wind. *Keel-dee-a, Keel-dee-a.* The surface of the land was as busy as a rough sea—it broke in sandstone outcrops, low buttes, ragged bluffs, hollow combers of bleached clay, and was fissured with waterless creek beds, ash-white, littered with boulders. Brown cows nibbled at their shadows on the open range. In the bottomlands, where muddy rivers trickled through the cottonwoods, were fenced rectangles of irrigated green.

Corn? wheat? alfalfa? Though I grew up in farmland, asthma and hayfever kept me at an allergic distance from crops and animals, and it was with the uninformed pleasure of the urban tourist that I watched this countryside unfold. I loved its dry, hillocky emptiness. To be so blessedly alone with it, so far from the nearest freeway and the nearest city, was a townee's holiday treat. Here were space and distance on a scale unimaginable to most city-dwellers. Here one might loaf and stretch and feel oneself expand to meet the enormous expanse of the land.

I stopped the car on the crest of a big swell and attacked a shrink-wrapped sandwich bought at a gas station several hours before. The smell of red dust, roasted, biscuity, mixed with the medicinal smell of the sage-brush that grew on the stony slopes of the buttes. I thought, I could spend all day just listening here—to the birds, the crooning wind, the urgent fiddling of the crickets.

The gas-station sandwich, with its washcloth turkey and distressed lettuce, was not a happy affair—and I gazed out of the window at a vision of *fegato alla salvia*. The calves and the sage were ready and waiting on the landscape, but it would take a 1,100-mile drive to Seattle in one direction or a 700-mile drive to

Opposite: a bankrupt farmer's possessions are sold off at a farm foreclosure auction.

Photo: Rob Amberg (Impact Visuals)

Minneapolis in the other to find an Italian restaurant to combine them on a menu. Here, where eastern Montana snugged into the corner made by Wyoming and the Dakotas, was the least populated, least visited region in all of the United States—a tract of rough pasture as big as England, on the western rim of the Badlands.

Mauvaises terres. The first missionary explorers had given the place its name, a translation of a Plains Indian term meaning something like hard-to-travel country, for its daunting walls and pinnacles and buttresses of eroded sandstone and sheer clay. Where I was now, in Fallon County, Montana, close to the North Dakota state line, the Badlands were getting better. A horseback rider wouldn't have too much difficulty getting past the blisters and eruptions that scarred the prairie here. But the land was still bad enough to put one in mind of Neil Armstrong and the rest of the Apollo astronauts: dusty, cratered, its green turning to sere yellow under the June sun.

The road ahead tapered to infinity, in stages. Hill led to hill led to hill, and at each summit the road abruptly shrank to half its width, then half its width again, until it became a hairline crack in the land, then a faint wobble in the haze, then nothing. From out of the nothing now came a speck. It disappeared. It resurfaced as a smudge, then as a fist-sized cloud. A while passed. Finally, on the nearest of the hilltops, a full-scale dust-storm burst into view. The storm enveloped a low-slung pick-up truck, which slowed and came to a standstill beside the car, open window to open window.

'Run out of gas?'

'No—' I waved the remains of the hideous sandwich. 'Just having lunch.'

The driver wore a ˜stetson, once white, which in age had taken on the colour, and some of the texture, of a ripe Gorgonzola cheese. Behind his head, a big-calibre rifle was parked in a gun-rack. I asked the man if he was out hunting, for earlier in the morning I'd seen herds of pronghorn antelope; they had bounded away from the car on spindly legs, the white signal-flashes on their rumps telegraphing *Danger!* to the rest. But no, he was on his way into town to go to the store. Around here,

men wore guns as part of their everyday uniform, packing
Winchesters to match their broad-brimmed hats and high-heeled
boots. While the women I had seen were dressed in nineties
clothes, nearly all the men appeared to have stepped off the set of
a period Western. Their quaint costume gave even the most
arthritic an air of strutting boyishness that must have been a trial
to their elderly wives.

'Missed a big snake back there by the crick.' He didn't look
at me as he spoke, but stared fixedly ahead, with the wrinkled
long-distance gaze that solo yachtsmen, forever searching for
landfall, eventually acquire.

'He was a real beauty. I put him at six feet or better. It's a
shame I didn't get him—I could have used the rattle off of that
fellow . . . '

With a blunt-fingered hand the size of a dinner plate, he
raked through the usual flotsam of business cards, receipts, spent
ball-points and candy wrappings that had collected in the fold
between the windshield and the dash. 'Some of my roadkills,' he
said. Half a dozen snake rattles, like whelk shells, lay bunched in
his palm.

'Looks like you have a nice little hobby there.'

'It beats getting bit.'

He seemed in no particular hurry to be on his way, and so I
told him where I came from, and he told me where he came from.
His folks had homesteaded about eight miles over in *that*
direction—and he wagged his hat brim southwards across a
treeless vista of withered grass, pink shale and tufty sage. They'd
lost their place back in the thirties. 'The dirty thirties.' Now he
was on his wife's folks' old place, a dozen miles up the road. He
had eleven sections up there.

A section is a square mile. 'That's quite a chunk of
Montana. What do you farm?'

'Mostly cattle. We grow hay. And a section and a half is
wheat, some years, when we get the moisture for it.'

'And it pays?'

'One year we make quite a profit, and the next year we go
twice as deep as that in the hole. That's about the way it goes,
round here.'

'That's the way farmers like to say it goes just about everywhere, isn't it?'

We sat on for several minutes in an amiable silence punctuated by the cries of the killdeer and the faulty muffler of the pick-up. Then the man said, 'Nice visiting with you,' and eased forward. In the rear-view mirror I watched his storm of dust sink behind the brow of a hill.

In the nineteenth century, when ships under sail crossed paths in mid-ocean, they 'spoke' each other with signal flags; then, if sea conditions were right, they hove to, lowered boats, and the two captains, each seated in his gig, would have a 'gam', exchanging news as they bobbed on the wavetops. In *Moby-Dick*, Melville devoted a chapter to the custom, which was evidently still alive and well on this ocean-like stretch of land. It was so empty that two strangers could feel they had a common bond simply because they were encircled by the same horizon. Here it was a hard and fast rule for drivers to slow down and salute anyone else whom they met on the road, and it was considered a courtesy to stop and say howdy. Fresh from the city, I was dazzled by the antique good manners of the Badlands.

I t had not always been so empty here.
The few working ranches were now separated from their neighbours by miles and miles of rough, ribbed, ungoverned country, and each ranch made as self-important a showing on the landscape as a battlemented castle. First, there was the elaborately painted mailbox—representing a plough, a wagon team, a tractor, a well-hung Hereford bull—set at the entrance to a gravel drive. A little way beyond it stood a gallows, with twenty-five-foot posts supporting an arched crosspiece emblazoned with the names of two or three generations of family members, along with the heraldic devices of the family cattle brands: numbers and letters, rampant and couchant—in western-talk, 'upright' and 'lazy'. In the far distance lay the ranch, its houses, barns and outbuildings screened by a shelter-belt of trees. *Trees!* Here, where almost no trees grew of their own accord except along the river bottoms, these domestic forests announced that their owners had water (and in the West, water has always meant status and power),

agricultural know-how and long occupancy of the land. I figured that you could easily arrive at an accurate estimate of a given family's income, character and standing in Montana just by looking at their shelter-belt. Some were no more than a threadbare hedge of sickly cottonwoods, but one or two were as tall and dense and green as a bluebell wood in spring.

The families were so few, their farms so unexpected and commanding, that they mapped the land, stamping it with their names, much as England used to be mapped by its cathedral cities. Here, where a crew of surly heifers blocked the road beside the creek, was Garber country. A barred, lazy 'A' and upright 'T' were burnt into the hide of each animal—the family brand of the Garbers ('Gene—Fernande—Warren—Bernie') whose grand ranch-entrance I had passed eight or nine miles back. I honked, and was met by a unanimous stare of sorrowing resentment, as if I were trying to barge my way through an important cow-funeral. When I gingerly nudged the car past their brown flanks, the cattle booed me for my profanation.

A mile on, more cattle, bullocks this time, scarred with the same bar-lazy AT. New names fell at long, slow intervals: Brown . . . Breen . . . Shumaker . . . Householder . . . Their estates were great, but bare and comfortless. It might be nice enough in June to look out from your window and know yourself to be the owner of all the dust, rock and parched grass that you could see, and more—but how would it be in January at minus-twenty-five degrees? Then, the sheer breadth and weight of the land would get to you. You could go crazy up there on your white hill, listening to the coyotes yodel. I thought, I'd settle for a more sociable berth, like being a lighthouse-keeper.

Not long ago, things had been altogether different. For every surviving ranch, I passed a dozen ruined houses. The prairie was dotted about with wrecks. Their windows, empty of glass, were full of sky. Strips of ice-blue showed between their rafters. Some had lost their footing and tumbled into their cellars. All had buckled under the drifting tonnage of Montana's winter snows, their joists and roof beams warped into violin curves. Skewed and splayed, the derelicts made up a distinctive local architecture, as redolent of their place as Norfolk flint or New England clapboard of theirs.

It took me a while to see the little hilltop graveyards. I had mistaken them for cattle pens. Fenced with barbed wire and juniper posts, each held ten or twelve rotting wooden crosses, with, here and there, a professionally chiselled undertaker's headstone. The names of the departed—Dietz, Hoglund, Grimshaw—didn't match the names on the gallows of the working farms. Save for the odd empty jamjar, the individual graves were untended, but someone kept the fences up and the grass neatly cut. I supposed that for farmers here it came with the territory—the job of looking after the dead strangers on your land.

Once the eye grew accustomed to the dizzying sweep and chop of the prairie and began to focus on its details, the whole country presented itself as a graveyard, it was so strewn with relics of the dead: single fenceposts, trailing a few whiskers of wire; the body of a Studebaker, vintage *circa* 1940, stripped of its wheels and engine, on a sandy knoll; a harrow, deep in the grass, its tines rusting to air; on the tops of the buttes, small cairns of carefully piled stones. For as far as one could see, and one could see further here than anywhere I'd ever been on land, the dead had left their stuff lying around, to dissolve back into nature in its own time, at its own pace. A civilization of sorts—houses, cars, machinery—was fading rapidly off the land, and it wouldn't be long before its imprint was as faint as that of the Plains Indians' teepee-rings or the shallow grooves worn by the single-file herds of buffalo.

I pulled up beside a wrecked house that stood conveniently close to the road and, stepping high and cautiously for fear of six-foot rattlers, made my way through the remains of the garden, past the assorted auto parts, the stoved-in chicken coops, the tin bath with a hole in its bottom, the wringer, the bedstead, the Frigidaire with the missing door. Though its frame had started to corkscrew, and its front wall bulged, the house was in better shape than most; a gabled two-storey cottage with a collapsed veranda, that in its day must have been as proudly, prettily suburban as any farmhouse on the prairie.

Inside, I was met by a panic scurry of wings: swallows had built their wattle-and-daub nests at picture height on the parlour walls. Squealing shrilly, the birds fled through the windows. It looked as if the owners had quit the place as precipitately as the swallows. They'd left most of their furniture to the mice, who'd nested in the sofa cushions, and the birds, who'd marbled the slip-covers with their droppings. A fly-swatter hung on its appointed nail. A foldaway ironing-board stood open, inviting the thought that perhaps the family had left the house in their Sunday best, outfacing the unkind world in freshly-pressed pants and blouses.

In the room beyond, I found clothes still hanging in the closet. Curious about their date and fashion, I reached for a dress, but the mildewed cotton came away in my hand like a fistful of spider's web. In the bottom of the closet stood a pair of cowboy boots. All day I'd felt in need of snakeboots, but these were a couple of sizes too large for me, and their leather was so cracked and stiff that it was well on its way to becoming fossilized.

Above each window in the house, the curtain rods had torn fringes of yellowed lace suspended from them. Four inches deep at best, these genteel remnants shivered in the wind. Lace curtains on the prairie . . . The woman who'd put them up had made a thorough job of her hemstitching: though the curtains themselves had rotted and blown out long ago, their stubs looked as if they might yet survive several more years of gales and blizzards. I could feel the woman's excitement at her handiwork as she veiled the buttes and outcrops with a pretty fall of white lace. The curtains would have altered the land for her as importantly as any amount of planting and ploughing.

The parlour floor was a sorry rubble of papers, books, magazines. Here, open on its title page, was the USDA *Yearbook of Agriculture* for 1935, badly foxed and swollen with damp. There was an ancient Montgomery Ward mail-order catalogue. I stirred the rubble with my shoe and came up with a mud-splattered postcard, mostly illegible. *Dear Neva, Hi Honey, what's the . . . with you, did you . . . or are you . . . we went fishing . . . if you have to go down to meet her . . . we went to the dance Monday . . . couldn't darn . . . Saturday . . .* In the corner behind the sofa I spotted a sheaf of manuscript pages. They had been chucked into the one dry spot in the room, which had otherwise been raked from end to end by rain and snow, and the ink on them was unsmudged. Perched on the sofa-arm, I settled down to read.

The densely-scribbled figures looked like prose, but were in fact an epic of desperate small-hours arithmetic—a sum that continued over seven pages of heavily-corrected addition and multiplication. The handwriting grew crankier, more bunched and downward-sloping, as the sum progressed and the numbers mounted. To begin with, it didn't look so bad. The amounts were small—$4.20, $9.15, $2.54—and they took time to swell up and burst. They sketched a careful life: rent to the Bureau of Land Management (the letters BLM were repeated several times and ringed in a blue doodle that went through the surface of the paper); payments to Sears, to Coast to Coast Hardware, to Kyle's Radiator Shop, to Lawler Drugs for animal vaccines, to J. T. Rugg for seeds, to Walter somebody for tractor tyres, to L. Price for a whole bunch of things, to Farmers Elevator, to Sinclair, Blacksmith, to Oscar Overland for oats, to Ward's and Hepperle's and Gamble's and Fullerton Lumber.

On the third page, a ringed figure showed for the first time: $1,040.40—'Note at Baker Bank.' The interest on this loan looked enviably low: at $40.50 for the year it came out at around four per cent. But even this was more than the family was spending on clothes ($35.51, with everything bought at J. C. Penney). $1,040.40. The horrible figure was written out several times in the margins, and islanded with shaky circles.

By the last page, the handwriting was all over the place, and the figures were standing, or leaning, an inch high on the paper. How do you turn $2.54 into $5,688.90? Easy. You just add and go on adding and adding, until you scare yourself sick. The document in my hands would drive anyone to the Jim Beam bottle. I've made my own pages of calculations in the same distraught writing; seen the numbers gang up on me and breed at a crazy rate. What the bottom line always comes to is the old two a.m. cry: *We can't go on living like this.*

The wind creaked in the roof. This house had been built to last. Its frames were stout, its cedar floor laid like a yacht's deck. It had been meant for the grandchildren and their children's children, and it must have seemed—when? in 1915? 1920?—a rock-solid investment: a fine house in the country, with a barn and outbuildings. Even now one could feel the pride of its owners

in their creation, though it had sunk in value to a few dollars' worth of firewood and a convenient nesting box for the neighbourhood birds.

A little further on, past another pocket-sized cemetery, stood a schoolhouse on a hill. Hay-bales were stacked in what had been the yard, between the trestle frame of the swings and the basketball hoop on its pole. Some flakes of whitewash still adhered to the bare grain of the wood on the schoolhouse wall. I stepped inside.

A dead woodpecker lay on the floor, and more swallows had built their mud-igloos on the walls, but the schoolroom retained the odour of morning milk, wet coats and spelling bees. The place had been heated by a great cast-iron stove, dusty and birdlimed now. In winter, it would have roared and crackled through the lessons, its voice as memorable to the students as that of the teacher. A framed sepia engraving of George

113

Washington (who could not tell a lie) hung over the blackboard, on which some recent visitor had left the chalked message, SPOKANE OR BUST!!!

The teacher's quarters were downstairs in the basement. Ice-heaves had wrecked the cement floor, but everything else was in place: the chaste single bed, the table and upright chair, the propane gas cooker, the rocker, with a maroon velvet cushion, for listening to the radio in the evenings over a mug of cocoa and a good book. The chest of drawers had been emptied, but there were three cardboard boxes of mouldering schoolbooks under the bed. Comfortably seated in Teacher's rocking chair, I leafed through her library. The books had been published between 1910 and the late thirties: grade-school readers, most of them put out by Ginn and Company, enshrining a version of America that now seemed hardly less distant than that of the Pilgrim Fathers—it was so bold and bright and innocent:

> Have you a flag hanging in your schoolroom? What are the colors in our flag? Many people think that these colors have a meaning.
>
> They think that the red in our flag means that we must be brave. They think that the blue in our flag means that we must be true. They think that the white means that we must be clean.
>
> How many stripes does our flag have? How many stars does it have?

A poem, printed in gothic script, nicely caught the mood of things:

> *A youth across the sea,*
> *   for the sake of a hope in his breast,*
> *Shook out a steadfast sail upon a dauntless quest.*
> *He had seen a star in the West,*
> *He had dreamed a dream afar;*
> *He wrought and would not rest.*
> *Heirs of that dream we stand,*
> *Citizens of that star—*
> *   America, dear land!*

I read stories about Washington and Betsy Ross, about the sickly boyhood of Theodore Roosevelt ('For years he had to sleep sitting up against some pillows. He could not lie down without coughing,') and the impoverished boyhood of Andrew Jackson ('But Andrew kept growing in spite of all they said. He clinched his little fists at colic, measles, and whooping cough. He talked very early, and walked instead of crawled . . . ').

From a useful book titled *Who Travels There*, I learned what to do when lost in the wilderness:

> If you ever find that you are lost, do not become frightened. There is more danger in fright than there is of starvation or accident. If you allow yourself to become frightened, you become possessed of what we call 'the panic of the lost'.
>
> As soon as you discover that you have lost your way in the wilderness, sit down with your back against a stump or stone, take out your jackknife and play mumblety-peg or sing a song. This will pull you together, so to speak. Then take a stick, smooth off a place in the dirt, and try to map out your wanderings. Making this map will cause you to remember forgotten objects you have passed on the road, and may help you to retrace your steps.

The America of the schoolbooks was a realm of lonely but invigorating adventure, where poor farm-boys grew up to be President; land of the brave, the true and the clean, where a beckoning star stood permanently above the western horizon and poverty and ill-health were tests of one's American mettle.

To prairie children, this schoolbook America must have seemed reasonably close to home. Its heroes were small farmers like their parents. There were no cities in it, and not a whiff from the smokestacks of heavy industry. Agriculture was everybody's business. Theodore Roosevelt's childhood (most of which had actually been spent on East Twentieth Street in Manhattan) was relocated, for story-book purposes, to the great outdoors, where little Theodore 'tried to take part in all the sports which other children took part in. He tried so hard that before he was a big boy he could swim and row and skate and box and shoot. He could ride horseback. He could sail a boat.' Beyond the village and the farm lay the wilderness, from which boys with jackknives learned to navigate their way home. The values honoured in the books—self-reliance, piety, woodcraft, patriotism—were all values that would come in handy in eastern Montana. Children in New York and Chicago, poring over the same texts, might as well have been reading about the land of Oz.

Here, though, you could see your own experience intimately reflected in the books. The Grade Three *Learn to Study* reader (1924) had a chapter titled 'How to Save':

> Have you ever tried to help your father and mother to save money? Some children think that they cannot save, because they are not working and earning money. You can save money by saving other things.

Good advice followed. Save your clothes: keep out of the mud; hang your things up when you take them off; use a napkin when you're eating; learn to sew on buttons. Mark your possessions: keep your rubbers fastened together with a clothespin; buy a ten-cent roll of adhesive tape and use it to put your name on your cap, gloves and boots; shave a strip off the top of your pencil and write your name there. Don't waste costly paper: if you want to draw a picture, do it on the back of a used sheet.

Thrift-conscious eight-year-olds, saving their parents' money with needle and thread and rolls of adhesive tape, were a type unfamiliar to me. Most of the eight-year-olds I knew were into Nintendo and hundred-dollar Raiders jackets. But it wasn't hard to imagine such an anxious and considerate child living in the house I had just left. He'd draw his pictures on the backs of old bills from Oscar Overland and J. T. Rugg.

The chapter on 'Buying Christmas Presents' gave one an idea of the kinds of luxuries that were within dreaming distance of a third-grader on the prairie: a spinning top (ten cents), a jackknife (thirty-eight cents), a striped ball (five cents), a toy automobile (sixty-five cents), a locomotive (one dollar) and—hope against hope!—way up on top of the list, a pair of skates for two dollars. The twelve designated presents came to a total of $5.68.

The coast was clear. Not a soul in sight, not a puff of dust on the far horizon. I loaded two armfuls of stolen books into the trunk of the car and headed south to Baker, where I put up in a motel room furnished with junk from the wilder reaches of the fifties. The pictures on its walls were all of water: two horseback explorers were in the act of discovering a mountain lake; a packhorse bridge spanned a river in what looked like Constable country; printed on dark blue velvet, a Japanese sea was in the grip of a *tsunami*. They were pictures for a dry country. At $23.50 for three beds, a bathroom and a fully equipped kitchen, the room was pleasingly in character with the frugal spirit of the place.

That evening a thunderstorm moved in on Baker from the West. One could see it coming for an hour before it hit: the distant artillery flashes on a sky of deep episcopal purple. As the storm advanced, I sat in a bar on Main Street, reading the life of Patrick Henry in *Four American Patriots: A Book for Young Americans* by Alma Holman Burton.

> 'Colonel Washington,' said Mr Davies, 'is only twenty-three years old. I cannot but hope that Providence has preserved the youth in so signal a manner for some important service to his country.'
>
> 'Ah,' thought Patrick, 'George Washington has done so much for his country, and he is only twenty-three!'

The people in the bar were huddled and talkative: living by day in so much space and solitude, they evidently liked to squash up close at night. At the back of the place, two poker tables were in session, the players gossiping unprofessionally between reckless bids of fifty cents a time. The slogan in scabbed paint on the bar door announced: LIQUOR UP FRONT, POKER IN THE REAR—an unsavoury old chestnut in Montana, where bars doubled as casinos.

> He looked down at his hands. They were brown and rough with toil.
>
> 'Alas!' he said, 'I do my best, and yet I cannot even make a living on my little farm!'
>
> This was quite true.
>
> Patrick could not make his crops grow. Then his

117

house caught fire and burned to the ground. It was all
very discouraging!

The snippets of bar conversation were, on the whole, more
interesting than Alma Holman Burton's prose. A Mexican seated
at the table next to me was talking to a scrawny, pencil-
moustached, thirtyish type, perched on a swivel-stool at the bar.
The Mexican said he was up in Baker from Wilmer, Texas.

'*Wilmer?*' said the guy at the bar, in a whoop of delighted
recognition. 'I know Wilmer! I was in jail in Wilmer. Buy you a
drink, man?'

> And so, at the age of twenty-three, Patrick Henry, with
> a wife and little children to provide for, did not have a
> shilling in his pocket. But his father helped a little, and
> Sarah's father helped a little, and they managed to keep
> the wolf from the door . . .

. . . which would not have been a dead metaphor to a child in
eastern Montana, where wolves picked off the sheep at nights
and 'wolfers' trapped the animals for bounty.

> 'There is one thing I can say about Patrick,' said Sarah's
> father; 'he does not swear nor drink, nor keep bad
> company.'

The thunder was directly overhead, and it was immediately
followed by a long kettledrum tattoo of rain on the roof. The bar
went quiet. Everyone in it listened to the rain.

'It's a gulleywasher,' the bartender said, gathering in the
empties.

The thunder rolled away eastwards, towards North Dakota,
but the rain kept coming.

'It's a gulleywasher,' said the man who'd done jail-time in
Wilmer, as if he had just minted the expression.

A crowd formed at the open doorway of the bar to watch
the downpour. The rain fell in gleaming rods. Main Street was a
tumbling river, already out of its banks and spilling over on to
the sidewalk. Its greasy waters were coloured red, white and blue
by the neon signs in the bar window. A truck sloshed past at

crawling-speed, throwing up a wake that broke against the doors of darkened stores.

'*That*,' said a turnip-faced old brute in a stetson, speaking in the voice of long and hard experience, 'is a gulleywasher.'

People craned to see. A couple had brought their toddler along (this was an easygoing bar in an easygoing town); the man lifted her on to his shoulders to give her a grandstand view of the wonder. The rain made everyone young: people dropped their guard in its presence, and the pleasure in their faces was as empty of self-consciousness as that of the toddler, who bounced against her father's neck, saying 'Water. Water. Water.' One man tried to launch a dry little joke at the rain's expense, but no one listened to him. Some shook their heads slowly from side to side, their faces possessed by the same aimless smile. Some whistled softly through their teeth. A woman laughed; a low, cigarette-stoked laugh that sounded uncannily like the hiss and crackle of the rain itself.

It went on raining. It was still raining when I drove back to the motel, where the forecourt was awash, and the kitchen carpet blackly sodden. I sat up listening to it, attuned now to what I ought to hear. When rain falls in these parts, in what used to be known as the Great American Desert, it falls with the weight of an astounding gift. It falls like money.

CHANG-RAE LEE
MY LOW KOREAN MASTER

For my father, the world—and by that I must mean this very land, the United States, his chosen nation—operated on a determined set of procedures, certain rules of engagement. These rules were the inalienable rights of the immigrant.

I was to inherit them, the legacy unfurling before me this way: you worked from sunrise to the dead of night. You were never unkind in your dealings, but neither were you generous. Your family was your life, though you rarely saw them. You kept handsome sums of cash close by in small denominations. You were steadily cornering the market in self-pride. You drove a Chevy and then a Caddy and then a Benz. You never missed a mortgage payment or a day of church. You prayed furiously until you wept. You considered the only unseen forces to be those of capitalism and the love of Jesus Christ. My father knew nothing of the mystical and the neurotic; they were not part of his make-up. They were for Americans, whom he considered crazy, self-indulgent, too rich in time and money.

My low Korean master. He died of a massive global stroke. It was the third one that finally killed him. My wife, Lelia, and I were going up on the weekends to help. We had retained a nurse to be there during the week.

He died during the night. In the morning I went to wake him, and his jaw was locked open, his teeth bared, cursing the end to its face. He was still gripping the knob of the brass bedpost, which he had bent at the joint all the way down to four o'clock. He was going to jerk the whole house over his head. Gritty mule. I thought he was never going to die. Even after the first stroke, when he had trouble walking and urinating and brushing his teeth, I saw him as a kind of ageing soldier, a squat, stocky-torsoed warrior, bitter, never self-pitying, fearful, stubborn, world fucking heroic.

We used to shower together when I was young; he would scrub my head so hard I thought he wanted my scalp, and rub his wide thumb against the skin of my forearms until the dirt would magically appear in tiny, black rolls. He would growl and hoot beneath the streaming water, and the dark hair between his legs would get soapy and white and make his genitals look like a soiled and drunken Santa Claus. When he needed cleaning after the strokes, he would let Lelia bathe him. He hated my helping him, especially in the bathroom. He would let her shampoo the coarse hair of his dense, unmagical head, wash his blue prick, but only if I was around. He said (my jaundiced translation of his Korean) that he didn't want me becoming *an anxious boy*, that I should be there: he knew all of my panic buttons, that craphound, inveterate sucker-puncher, that damned machine.

The second stroke, just a week before the last one, took away his ability to move or speak. He sat up in bed with those worn, black eyes and had to listen to me talk. I don't think he had ever heard so much from my mouth. I talked straight through the night, and he silently took my confessions, maledictions, as though he were some font of blessing at which I might leave a final, belated tithe. I spoke at him, this propped-up father figure, half-intending an emotional torture. I ticked through the whole long register of my disaffections, hit all the ready categories. I berated him for the way he had conducted his life with my mother, and his businesses and beliefs, to speak once and for all the less than holy versions of who he was.

I thought he would be an easy mark, being stiff, paralysed, but of course the agony was mine. He was unmoveable. I thought, too, that he was mocking me with his mouth, which lay slack, agape. Nothing I said seemed to penetrate him. But then what was my speech? He had raised me in a foreign land, put me through college, witnessed my marriage, even left me enough money that I could do the same for my children without the expense of his kind of struggle; his duties, uncomplex, were by all accounts complete. And the single-minded determination that had propelled him through twenty-five years of greengrocering in a famous ghetto of America would serve him a few last days, and through any of my meagre execrations.

I thought his life was all about money. He drew much energy and pride from his ability to make it almost at will. He was like some kind of human annuity. He had no real cleverness or secrets for good business; he simply refused to fail, leaving absolutely nothing to luck or chance or someone else. Of course, in his personal lore he would have said that he started with $200 in his pocket and a wife and baby and just a few words of

English. Knowing what every native loves to hear, he would have offered the classic immigrant story, casting himself as the heroic newcomer, self-sufficient, resourceful.

The truth, though, is that my father got his first infusion of capital from a *ggeh*, a Korean 'money club' in which members contributed to a pool that was given out on a rotating basis. Each week you gave the specified amount; one week in the cycle, all the money was yours.

His first *ggeh* was formed from a couple dozen storekeepers who knew each other through a fledgling Korean–American business association. In those early days he would take me to their meetings down in the city, a third-floor office in midtown, Thirty-Second Street between Fifth and Broadway, where the first few Korean businesses opened in Manhattan in the mid 1960s. On the block then were just one grocery, two small restaurants, a custom tailor and a bar. At the meetings the men would be smoking, talking loudly, almost shouting their opinions. There were a few arguments, but mostly it was just hope and excitement. I remember my father as the funny one; he'd make them all laugh with an old Korean joke or his impressions of Americans who came into his store, doing their stiff nasal tone, their petty annoyances and complaints.

In the summers we'd all get together, these men and their families, drive up to Westchester to some park in Mount Kisco or Rye. In the high heat, the men would set up cones and play soccer, and even then I couldn't believe how hard they tried and how competitive they were, my father especially, who wasn't so much skilled as ferocious, especially in defence. He'd tackle his good friend, Mr Oh, so hard that I thought a fight might start, but then Mr Oh was gentle and quick on his feet and he'd pull up my father and just keep working to the goal.

Sometimes they would team up and play some Hispanic men who were also picnicking with their families. Once, they even played some black men, though my father pointed out to us in the car on the way home that they were *African* blacks. Somehow there were rarely white people in the park, never groups of their families, just young couples, sometimes. After iced barley tea and a quick snack, my father and his friends would set up a volleyball net and start all over again. The mothers and we younger ones would sit and watch, the older kids playing their own games, and when the athletics were done, the mothers would set up the food and grill the ribs and the meat, and we'd eat and run and play until dark. When my father dumped the water from the cooler, it was the sign that we would go home.

Over the years, my father and his friends got together less and less. After my mother died, he didn't seem to want to go to the gatherings any more. But it wasn't just him. His friends got busier and wealthier and lived further and further apart. Like us, their families moved to big houses with big yards to tend on weekends; they owned fancy cars that needed washing and waxing. They joined their own neighbourhood pool and tennis clubs and were making drinking friends with Americans. Some of them, too, were already dead, like Mr Oh, who had a heart attack after being held up at his store in Hell's Kitchen. And in the end, my father no longer belonged to any *ggeh*; he complained about all the disgraceful troubles that were now cropping up, people not paying on time or leaving too soon after their turn getting the money. In America, he said, it's even hard to stay Korean.

I wonder if my father, given the chance, would have wished to go back to the time before he made all that money, when he had just one store and we rented a tiny apartment in Queens. He worked hard and had worries but he had a joy then that he never seemed to regain once the money started coming in. He might turn on the radio and dance cheek to cheek with my mother. He worked on his car himself, a used green Impala with carburettor trouble. They had lots of Korean friends that they met at church and then even in the street, and when they talked in public there was a shared sense of how lucky they were, to be in America but still have countrymen near.

I know he never felt fully comfortable in his fine house in Ardsley. Though he was sometimes forward and forceful with neighbours, he mostly operated as if the town were just barely tolerating our presence. The only time he'd come out in public was because of me. He would steal late and unnoticed into the gym where I was playing kiddie basketball and stand by the far side of the bleachers with a rolled-up newspaper in his hand, tapping it nervously against his thigh as he watched the action, craning to see me shoot the ball but never shouting or urging like the other fathers and mothers did.

My mother was even worse, and she would ruin a birthday cake rather than bear the tiniest shame—asking her next-door neighbour and friend for an egg or the child's pinch of baking powder.

I remember thinking, *what's she afraid of?* Why did we have to be so careful of what people thought of us, as if we ought mince delicately about our immaculate neighbourhood, we silent partners of the bordering WASPs and rich Jews? We never rubbed them except with a smile, as if everything with us were always fine, our great sham of propriety, as if nothing could wreak anger or sadness upon us. Did we always have to demonstrate our belief in anything American, in impressing Americans, in making money, polishing apples in the dead of night, perfectly pressed pants, perfect credit, being perfect, shooting black people in the back, watching our stores and offices burn down to the ground?

Then, inevitably, if I asked hard questions of myself, what might I come up with?

What belief did I ever have in my father, whose daily life I so often ridiculed and looked upon with such abject shame? The summer before I started high school, he made me go with him to one of the new stores on Sunday afternoons to help restock the shelves and the bins. I hated going. My friends—suddenly including some girls—were always planning tennis or trips to the pool club. I never told them why I couldn't go. Later I found out from one of them that they simply thought I was religious.

When working in the store, I wore a white apron over my slacks and dress shirt and tie. The store was on Madison Avenue, in the eighties, and my father made all the employees dress up for the blue-haired matrons and the fancy dogs, and the sensible young mothers pushing antique velvet-draped prams containing the most quiet of infants, and the banker fathers, brooding, annoyed, aloof and humourless.

My father, thinking it might be good for business, urged me

to show them how well I spoke English, casually to recite 'some Shakespeare words'.

I, his princely Hal. Instead, and only in part to spite him, I grunted my best Korean to the other men. I saw that if I just kept speaking the language of our work, the customers didn't seem to see me. I wasn't there. They didn't look at me. I was an unthreatening shadow. I could even catch a rich old woman, whose tight strand of pearls pinched in the sags of her neck, whispering to her friend right behind me, 'Oriental Jews.'

I never retaliated or said anything smart like, 'Does madam need help?' I kept on stacking the hothouse tomatoes and Bosc pears. That same woman came in the store every day; once, I saw her take a small bite of an apple and then put it back with its wound facing down. I started over to her, not knowing what I might say, when my father intercepted me and said in Korean, smiling, as if he were complimenting me, 'She's a steady customer.' He nudged me back to my station. I had to wait until she left before I could replace the ruined apple with a fresh one.

I threw most of my frustration into building perfect, truncated pyramids of fruit. The other two workers, whom I knew as Mr Yoon and Mr Kim, seemed to have even more bottled up inside them, their worries of money and family. They marched through the work as if they wanted to deplete themselves of all their energy, of all their means of struggle. They peeled and sorted and bunched and sprayed and cleaned and stacked and shelved and swept; my father put them to any task as long as it meant they didn't have to speak. They both had college degrees, were recent immigrants in their thirties with wives and young children, knew no one in the country and spoke hardly any English. They worked twelve-hour days six days a week for $200 cash and meals and all the fruit and vegetables we couldn't or wouldn't sell; it was the typical arrangement. My father, like all successful immigrants before him, gently and not so gently exploited his own.

'This is way I learn business, this is way they learn business.'

And although I knew he gave them a hundred-dollar bonus every now and then, I never let on that I felt he was anything but cruel to his workers. I still imagine Mr Kim's and Mr Yoon's

Every issue of Granta features fiction, travel writing, autobiography, reportage and more. So don't miss out — subscribe today and save up to 40% on the £7.99 cover price.

Don't miss out on major issues. Subscribe now to Granta and save up to 40%.

If I subscribe for 3 years, I save £38.38. (That's 40%.)

I want to take out a subscription (4 issues a year) to Granta.

❏ 1 yr £21.95 ❏ 2 yrs £41.00 ❏ 3 yrs £57.50.

Start my subscription with issue number _____.

Payment: ❏ Cheque, payable to 'Granta'
❏ Access/MasterCard/American Express/Visa

Expiry Date _____

❏❏❏❏❏❏❏❏❏❏❏❏❏❏❏❏❏❏

Signature _____

Overseas postage:
There is no additional postage for UK subscriptions.
For Europe (including Eire), please add £8 a year.
For overseas, please add £15 a year.

❏ Please tick this box if you do not wish to receive occasional mailings from other organizations and publications that may be of interest to you.

I want to give a one-year, £21.95 gift subscription.

My name:

Name _____

Address _____

_____

Postcode _____

Payment: ❏ Cheque, payable to 'Granta'
❏ Access/MasterCard/American Express/Visa

Expiry Date _____

❏❏❏❏❏❏❏❏❏❏❏❏❏❏❏❏❏❏

Signature _____

£_____total for _____ gift subscriptions.

The gift(s) are for:

Name _____

Address _____

_____

Postcode _____
94M5S49B

Overseas postage:
There is no additional postage for UK subscriptions.
For Europe (including Eire), please add £8 a year.
For overseas, please add £15 a year.

Don't let your friends miss out either. One year gifts (4 issues) are only £21.95.

FREEPOST
2-3 Hanover Yard
Noel Road
London
N1 8BR

FREEPOST
2-3 Hanover Yard
Noel Road
London
N1 8BR

children, lonely for their fathers, gratefully eating whatever was brought home to them, our overripe and almost rotten mangoes, our papayas, kiwis, pineapples, these exotic tastes of their wondrous new country, this joyful fruit now too soft and too sweet for those who knew better, us near natives, us earlier Americans.

I made endless fun of the prices of my father's goods, how everything ended in .95 or .98 or .99.

'Look at all the pennies you need!' I'd cry when the store was empty, holding up the rolls beneath the cash register. 'It's so ridiculous!'

He'd cry back, 'What you know? It's good for selling!'

'Who told you that?'

He was wiping down the glass fronts of the refrigerators of soda and beer and milk. 'Nobody told me that. I know automatic. Like everybody else.'

'So then why is this jar of artichoke hearts three ninety-eight instead of three ninety-nine?'

'You don't know?' he said, feigning graveness.

'No, Dad, tell me.'

'Stupid boy,' he answered, clutching at his chest. His overworked merchant heart. 'It's feeling.'

I remember when my father would come home from his vegetable stores late at night, and my mother would say the same three things to him as she fixed his meal of steamed barley rice and beef flank soup: *Spouse*, she would say, *you must be hungry. You come home so late. I hope we made enough money today.*

She never asked about the stores themselves, about what vegetables were selling, how the employees were working out, nothing, ever, about the painstaking, plodding nature of the work. Maybe she simply didn't care to know the particulars, but when I asked him one night about the business (I must have been six or seven), my mother immediately called me back into the bedroom and closed the door.

'Why are you asking him about the stores?' she interrogated me in Korean, plaintive, edgy, as though she were in some pain.

'I was just asking,' I said.

'Don't ask him. He's very tired. He doesn't like talking about it.'

'Why not?' I said, louder this time.

'Shh!' she said, grabbing my wrists. 'Don't shame him! Your father is very proud. You don't know this, but he graduated from the best college in Korea, the very top, and he doesn't need to talk about selling fruits and vegetables. It's below him. He only does it for you, Byong-ho, he does everything for you. Now go and keep him company.'

I walked back to the living-room and found my father asleep on the sofa, his round mouth pursed, his breath filtering softly through his nose. A single fruit fly, its armoured back an ugly, metallic green, was dancing a circle on his chin. What he'd brought home from work.

Once, he came home with deep bruises about his face, his nose and mouth bloody, his rough workshirt torn at the shoulder. He smelled rancid as usual from working with vegetables, but more so that night, as if he'd fallen into the compost heap. He came in and went straight up to the bedroom and shut and locked the door. My mother ran to it, pounding on the wood and sobbing for him to let her in so she could help him. He wouldn't answer. She kept hitting the door, asking him what had happened, almost kissing the panels, the side jamb. I was too frightened to go to her. After a while she grew tired, and crumpled there, weeping, until finally he turned the lock and let her in. I went to my room where I could hear him talk through the wall. His voice was quiet and steady. Some black men had robbed the store and taken him to the basement and bound him and beaten him up. They took turns whipping him with the magazine of a pistol. They would have probably shot him right there, in the head, but his partners came for the night shift, and the robbers fled.

I learned later on that he had trained as an industrial engineer and completed a master's degree. I never learned the exact reason he chose to come to America. He once mentioned something about the 'big network' in Korean business, how someone from the rural regions of the country could only get so far in Seoul. I wondered whether he had assumed he could be an American engineer who spoke little English, but of course he couldn't.

He never asked me point-blank about work. He'd just inquire if I was earning enough for my family and then silently nod. He couldn't care for the importance of *career*. That notion was too costly for a man like him.

He genuinely liked Lelia. This surprised me. He was nice to her. When we met him at one of his stores he always had a basket of treats for her, trifles from his shelves, bars of dark chocolate, exotic tropical fruits, tissue-wrapped *biscotti*. He would show her around every time as if it were her first, introduce her to the day manager and workers, most of whom were Korean, tell them proudly in English that she was his daughter. He always tried to stand right next to her and would then marvel at how tall and straight she was, *like a fine young horse*, he'd say in Korean, admiringly. He'd hug her and ask me to take pictures. Laugh and kid with her generously.

He never said it, but I knew he liked the fact that Lelia was white. When I first told him that we were engaged, I thought he would vehemently protest, go over the scores of reasons why I should marry one of our own (as he had rambled on in my adolescence), but he only nodded and said he respected her and wished me luck. I think he had come to view our union logically, practically, and perhaps he thought he saw through my intentions, the assumption being that Lelia and her family would help me make my way in the land.

'Maybe you not so dumb after all,' he said to me after the wedding ceremony.

Lelia, an old-man lover if ever there was one, always said he was sweet.

Sweet.

'He's just a more brutal version of you,' she told me that last week we were taking care of him. 'It's refreshing.'

I didn't argue with her. My father was obviously not modern, in the psychological sense. He was mostly unencumbered by those needling questions of existence and self-consciousness. Irony was always lost on him. His was the definition of a thick skin. For most of my youth, I wasn't sure that he had the capacity to love. He showed great respect to my mother to the day she died, practised for her the deepest sense of duty and

131

honour, but I never witnessed from him a devotion I could call love. He never kissed her hand or bent down before her. He never said the word, in any language. Maybe none of this matters. But then I don't think he ever wept for her, either, even at the last moment of her life. I was ten. He came out of the hospital room from which he had barred me and said that she had passed, and I should go in and look at her one last time. I don't now remember what I saw in her room. Maybe I never actually looked at her. What I remember is my father standing there in the hall when I came back out, his hands clasped at his groin in a military pose, his neck taut and thick, working, trying hard to swallow the nothing balling up in his throat.

His life didn't seem to change. He seemed instantly recovered. The only noticeable thing was that he would come home much earlier than usual, at four in the afternoon instead of the usual eight or nine. He said he didn't want me coming home from school to an empty house, though he didn't actually spend any more time with me. He just went down to his workshop in the basement or to the garage to work on his car. For dinner we went either to a Chinese place or the Indian one in the next town, and sometimes he drove to the city so we could eat Korean. He settled us into a routine this way, a schedule. I thought all he wanted was to have nothing unusual sully his days, that what he disliked or feared most was uncertainty.

I wondered, too, whether he was suffering inside, whether he sometimes cried, as I did, for reasons unknown. I remember how I sat with him in those restaurants, both of us eating without savour, unjoyous, and my wanting to show him that I could be as steely as he, my chin as rigid and unquivering as any of his displays, that I would tolerate no mysteries either, no shadowy wounds or scars of the heart.

HELEN EPSTEIN
FAT

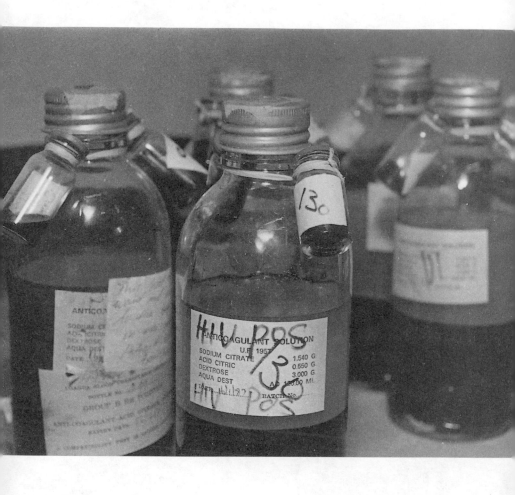

About two weeks before I was supposed to leave for Uganda, I packed up the materials I would need for the project I planned to do there and called Dr Arthur Murray, whom I would be working with, to confirm the shipping address.

'Maybe you shouldn't send the stuff just yet,' he said.

'There's a problem?'

'There may be a problem.'

'Is it a bad problem?'

'It could be.'

'Is it a political problem?'

'Well, it's not the whole country.'

'Just the project.'

'Yeah, just the project.'

A few days later he called and said that everything was OK; the problem had had to do with a truck.

'A truck?'

'Yeah. A truck.'

I knew it couldn't be so simple.

I arrived at Entebbe airport on a small propeller-driven plane from Nairobi and walked across the Tarmac to a two-storey concrete building that had been almost completely gutted. The only light came through the doorway; fragments of electrical wiring and old plumbing fixtures, black with tar and dirt, dangled from the walls and ceiling. A man lounged on an elevated platform; a sign above his head said HEALTH. This was the man who checked your immunization papers. To be allowed past him, you needed to show that you'd had injections for yellow fever, cholera and typhoid. Malaria pills and injections for meningitis, hepatitis A and B and rabies were also recommended.

Arthur was there to meet me. During the drive to Kampala, we talked about my materials, which hadn't arrived. I had called the shippers before I left, and they told me that they thought a project called CHIPS was closing and, thinking that my project was part of CHIPS, hadn't sent anything out for me. I told the shippers to send my parcels anyway, but what was this thing about CHIPS?

The names of the doctors in Uganda have been changed.

Photo: Mike Goldwater (Network)

135

When I asked him, Arthur became very tense. 'Just don't talk about that.'

So I didn't.

It was midday. I had been up all night in the airplane, and Africa seemed part of a waking dream. Soldiers in baggy, green uniforms, carrying huge machine-guns, shambled by on the road. We passed a sparkling lake, and a bright yellow bird flew up out of a field. I made myself a promise, which I would soon break, to learn the name of every plant and animal I saw. In town a cow stood on the grassy island in the centre of a roundabout surrounded by traffic.

I was taken to the house of Dr Celeste Quinn, on the campus of Makerere University where I would be living. Dr Quinn was a gynaecologist working with the urban poor in Kampala. She was also, I would learn later, the director of CHIPS, the internationally-funded medical project that I was discouraged from talking about.

Like most of the expatriate residences in Kampala, Dr Quinn's big, ranch-style house was a space-pod of western comfort. She had guards, servants, a telephone, a television. She was a heavy, slightly intimidating woman in a blue skirt and a blue-and-white polka-dot blouse. She had straight brown hair, small, grey eyes and scrubbed, white hands. When we were introduced, she extended a large, ivory arm and gave me a brief smile.

She was seeing off some friends at the door and seemed distracted, so I sat in a wicker chair on the sunny veranda and played with her cat which emerged from its cardboard box and slunk over to me. I lifted it off its front paws, and it arched its elastic body and passively looked me in the eye.

I would be working in an immunology lab at the Uganda Cancer Institute, a compound of one-storey, weathered concrete buildings with corrugated-iron roofs located in the grounds of Mulago Hospital, the only state-run hospital in Kampala. My lab was next to the dental clinic, and, although I later got used to it, the screams of the children being treated there could be heard all day.

The Cancer Institute has two barn-like, open wards, so dark and overcrowded that most of the patients and their families lounge on the verandas outside. They bathe their children under the outdoor spigot or prepare maize-meal and mashed bananas on open, wood fires. In the Mulago Hospital grounds I saw people with growths on their necks the size of pineapples and people without arms or legs. I saw someone without a nose.

My lab was on a gravelly slope above the Institute. Arthur took me there the day after I arrived and led me through the main lab, which was well-lit and crowded with equipment and technicians. We then passed into another, much smaller room, dark and full of cardboard boxes and rusty machine parts. When we pushed the door open, plumes of red African dust rose and swirled around us.

'We were thinking of putting you here,' Arthur told me. It was clear some other place would have to be found for the boxes and machine-parts. A plasterer would have to be hired, as well as someone to paint the room. We would then have to install a refrigerator and an overhead light. We would also have to find some kind of work surface, if only a table. Some time would pass before I could begin work.

A few days later, a contractor was hired, but he quarrelled with the Institute's chief accountant over how much the job would cost. The two men negotiated to within five dollars of each other, before the contractor got angry and left. It took days to get him to come back and accept his own terms.

In the meantime, I did not mind the delay. It coincided neatly with my continuing failure to locate the materials I had shipped out from California. I had contacted the shipping company which assured me that the boxes had been sent. They should have arrived. I called the airline, which said the packages were with customs; customs said the packages were with the clearing agent; and the clearing agent said the packages were with me.

The mystery left me with time for reflection. I am in general an impatient person and this kind of thing would ordinarily drive me mad. But for some reason it didn't. The problem took on a different scale, and the whereabouts of my boxes replaced the design of the ideal HIV vaccine as my primary obsession.

I had come to Kampala to do work that would contribute, I hoped, to developing a vaccine to protect Ugandans from infection with Human Immunodeficiency Virus (HIV), the virus that causes Acquired Immune Deficiency Syndrome (Aids). I became interested in the problem while doing post-doctoral work in California. I had been studying the sexual organs of a tiny insect the size of the 'I' in ELIZABETH on an English penny, when I looked up one day, unable to concentrate. That day a scientist named Kathy Steimer gave a talk about the HIV vaccine that had been developed in her lab in San Francisco. It had been injected into about two hundred volunteers. The results, so far, were encouraging.

After the lecture I never seriously returned to the world of the insect. My work had been bothering me for a long time. In the research being carried out at the university and in other places like it, 'frontiers' were the thing. It was unfashionable to study anything for a practical reason. We thought of ourselves as the astronauts of the cell, exploring the logic left behind by evolution's intricate digressions. Our heroes were the men and women who described the structure of the gene, saw the first microtubule and found out what ribosomes did. We were not in the business of making cures.

My academic outpost near San Francisco was some distance from the frontier. In the twenties a German scientist had observed that if you stained the nucleus of certain insect cells and looked at them under a light microscope, you saw a black dot. He wrote a series of long monographs on the subject, guessed that the black dot was a chromosome and left it to posterity to figure out what it was for.

My boss believed that the black dot had enormous significance, and we spent hours in his office, surrounded by doughnut boxes, discussing it. He liked doughnuts. He also liked crisps, cakes, sweets of every description and chewing-gum. He ate constantly, and his office was a library of junk food. For him, the black dot explained so many things. It determined sex, it was genetic memory, it was the death clock.

The bug we were studying was tiny, round and had six legs, each consisting of three segments. It had a pair of short antennae with seven segments and a tiny mandible. Its little body was covered with pores from which it secreted a pale goo in which it hid.

I once asked my boss if we shouldn't be out helping the poor and the sick, rather than searching for the meaning of a dot inside a bug that was almost too small to see.

'The poor and the sick will always be with us,' he said, 'but we will change the way people think about the world.'

He had a point, I suppose. But when I looked around me and saw a lab full of people muttering recondite gene-speak under their breath like prayers, it all began to seem very strange.

I longed for a biological problem that had meaning outside the world of the lab. I had known several people who had died of Aids. Most were young; all suffered horribly. Although thousands of scientists had spent billions of dollars trying to explain HIV, and the virus can now be described in almost atomic detail, nothing, as yet, can be done to stop it.

I asked a doctor who had worked on Aids in East Africa if he thought a molecular biologist might be useful there. He suggested that I write to a professor in San Francisco who was conducting a study of sexually-transmitted diseases in Uganda; perhaps this man would be able to give me some advice. I wrote to the professor and phoned his secretary some time in August. She told me he was very busy, but had time to see me at eleven-thirty on 23 October for a few minutes.

Professor Cornelius was about fifty, a round, little man with a tennis-ball fuzz of hair around his cheery face.

'So, you want to go to Africa!' he boomed. He rhapsodized about the poignant beauty of Kampala; the crowded, dirty city; the skeletal remains of the stone buildings downtown gutted by war; the surrounding hills and the vast slums in the folds of land between them; and about Makerere University and Mulago Hospital, once among the most distinguished in Africa, destroyed by Idi Amin, Milton Obote and twenty-five years of corruption and neglect.

In contrast to the West—where HIV is transmitted most often by sex between gay men or by needle-sharing among drug users—HIV in Uganda is transmitted mainly by sex between men and women. When western governments first recognized the magnitude of the Aids crisis there, they feared that this great plague affecting heterosexuals would spread northwards, and responded by pouring money into research. Professor Cornelius was among those now looking for an explanation for the epidemic among heterosexuals in Africa. He and others believed that the reason for it lay in the prevalence of sexually-transmitted diseases there. These diseases are thought to create conduits through which HIV moves from person to person. HIV-infected cells and virus particles do not penetrate unbroken skin and do not survive outside the body for more than a few seconds; to pass from one person to another, they must encounter either blood or damaged mucous membranes—the slimy surfaces of the body's internal cavities such as the vagina or the rectum. Sexually-transmitted diseases—gonorrhea, syphilis, chancroid, candida, herpes, venereal warts and others—cause genital sores and ulcers that provide broad, open avenues to the bloodstream. Diseases of this kind have always been widespread in East Africa; even though effective drugs are available, most people in poor, underdeveloped countries cannot afford them.

The professor was overseeing many projects pertaining to sexually-transmitted diseases in Uganda. One project—CHIPS, the thing I was later discouraged from talking about—was being run from Kampala by two of his young colleagues, Doctors Arthur Murray and Celeste Quinn. In the course of their work, they had collected blood from thousands of patients at a public sexually-transmitted-disease clinic in Kampala, but hadn't studied the samples, which were now stored in a freezer. The patients had been interviewed about their age, sex, tribe, religion, occupation, income, number of wives and sexual partners, years and types of sexual activity and current symptoms. Many of the responses were stored on a computer. About half the patients had been HIV positive.

Perhaps this was something I would like to work on?

We discussed possible experiments. Everyone knew about the epidemic in Uganda; a third of the population of the capital was thought to be infected. Here was a chance to work with samples of HIV about which very little was known. Although I wouldn't be paid—apart from my laboratory expenses—and wouldn't be officially a member of his staff in Kampala, I nevertheless saw this as a chance to do something practical with what I knew about biology.

The meeting with the professor was interrupted by an urgent phone call, and the secretary appeared at the door making cryptic gestures and mouthing things I wasn't supposed to understand.

2

I had been in Kampala for three weeks. The plasterer had fixed up my little lab; he painted it salmon pink. I still needed a refrigerator, and the Cancer Institute's accountant authorized the money for it. Viki, the pretty and very large Ugandan woman who ran the Institute storeroom, said she would help me. She warned me about the tendency of Ugandan salesmen to double the price of anything a white person buys. She recommended that we go see the Asians.

Traders from the Far and Middle East have been coming to East Africa for nearly two thousand years. Until recently, they ran most of Uganda's businesses, factories and the sugar and cotton plantations; they built many of the towns, taught in the university and owned a great deal of property. In 1972 Idi Amin threw them all out and gave their property to black Ugandans. Yoweri Museveni, president since 1986, offered the Asians the chance to return and reclaim their houses, shops and offices. Many have come back.

The Asians' shop was small and crowded, but the man behind the counter—a solid, little man with a very loud voice—seemed to know Viki, so we didn't have to wait long. He showed us something called a Sno-Cap.

'How much?' Viki asked.

'Twelve hundred.'

'Eight.'

'No.'

Silence. 'OK, eleven hundred and fifty.'

'Nine.'

'No.'

'Come on. Nine hundred.'

'Eleven hundred and that's as low as I can go.'

Viki looked at me. I nodded my assent.

'OK,' she said.

The refrigerator arrived at the lab a few days later. It was half the size of the one we had bought in the shop.

My boxes were still missing. I consulted Dr Quinn, who was full of sage advice about what to do. In the two years she had worked in Africa, she had seen this kind of thing happen a thousand times. She told me to check at the airport, the clearing agent and all around the hospital. She said that sometimes things just vanished; it was a chaotic world out here.

Dr Quinn—Celeste, she said I should call her—had something to confide in me, too. She was worried about the project she was running, CHIPS. The initials stood for Community Health Initiative for the Prevention of Sexually-transmitted diseases—a one-and-a-half-million-dollar project that was being funded by the United States Agency for International Development (USAID), a branch of the State Department.

As the director, Celeste had made the original application for funding—Professor Cornelius had offered advice and approval—and then had gone on to hire most of the 132 Ugandan staff.

The CHIPS project had been running for about a year and was located in a Kampala slum called Kisenyi, which means 'swamp' in Swahili. Kisenyi is located between two hills, where two of Kampala's many cathedrals stand. Catholic and Protestant missionaries brought Christianity to Uganda in the 1870s, and within ten years the converts were involved in a war that would last twelve years. Thousands were killed. Kampala's Catholic and Protestant cathedrals now face each other from adjacent hills, and Kisenyi lies in the depression between them. When it rains, the garbage and silt run down the hills and collect in Kisenyi. The air smells of rotting bananas and sewage. Children gather food from garbage tips, and rivulets of sludge course through the narrow passageways that serve as streets.

Kisenyi is where people displaced by war or poverty in other parts of the country end up when they come to Kampala. Some move on, some stay, many die. Everyone is poor and unemployed, and yet everyone appears to work. The men fix bicycles, build things out of wood, or steal. The women sell things: roasted bananas, cigarettes, sweets, themselves. The prevalence of both sexually-transmitted diseases and HIV infection is very high. CHIPS was established to see what effect a neighbourhood sexually-transmitted disease clinic and HIV-testing centre would have.

CHIPS was typical of most aid projects in Africa, being an uneasy collaboration between three parties with different interests: USAID, which provided the money; Dr Quinn, who was responsible for spending it; and the people of Kisenyi on whom the money was to be spent.

USAID's interest in all this was governed by its current goals, determined by the State Department, to combat Aids and other sexually-transmitted diseases and to promote family planning in developing countries. The aim was to achieve this almost entirely through a single instrument: the condom. The Agency financed a Ugandan condom-manufacturer and distributed condoms to hospitals and clinics around the country. Its ambition was to establish clinics dedicated to family planning and the control of sexually-transmitted diseases in slums all over the world. USAID had a lot of money to spend (its annual budget in Uganda alone was twenty million dollars), and it had, therefore, considerable power, if only in the number of people it gave jobs to: hundreds of American experts—in public health, education, waste management—who, in turn, hired thousands of local people. The Agency's aims were, fairly or not, invariably thought to be politically determined, and its policies had often been controversial.

The interests of the people of Kisenyi were very different: they were happy to receive free condoms, but what they really wanted were doctors and medicine. Even though the CHIPS clinic was dedicated to sexually-transmitted diseases, its clientele consisted not only of gonorrhea and syphilis patients, but of sufferers of every kind: children with measles, pneumonia, diarrhoea and malaria, as well as adults with Aids.

Celeste was in the difficult position of having to mediate between these interests. She saw the wisdom of promoting the use of condoms, but as a scientist she wanted to measure the effect condoms had in controlling sexually-transmitted diseases and the spread of HIV. She wanted to know which diseases were most common in Kisenyi as well as the best and cheapest ways of treating them. Such a project might seem simple, but she must have encountered many frustrations along the way. I can barely begin to imagine all the things that could have gone wrong.

At Mulago hospital, down the hill from where I worked, an American doctor was trying to determine how to treat cryptococcal meningitis, which often affects those in the last stages of Aids. He was ordinarily a mild man, who confronted Africa's inconveniences with wry amusement. But when I asked if I could accompany him on his rounds, he agreed only reluctantly and seemed irritated. I asked if anything was wrong.

'You'll see,' he said.

Cryptococcal meningitis is caused by a fungus that infects the fluid bathing the brain and spinal column. Everyone is exposed to the germ that causes the disease; its spores can be found on the leaves of certain trees or in the air. With few exceptions, however, the only people who get sick are those whose immune systems have collapsed to such an extent that they can't fight it off. The symptoms are nausea, vomiting, disorientation and headaches so severe that when a child dies of Aids in Uganda it is often said that he died of headache.

In Uganda the only treatment available was a highly toxic medicine that, even in moderate doses, caused permanent kidney damage. The drug the doctor was studying was not as toxic, but it was expensive. It was provided free to all patients who wished to participate in his study. Because all the patients had Aids, however, even those who were cured would die within a few years.

Following the doctor on his rounds, I was not surprised by the chipped paint and grimy windows, the torn, dirty sheets and the few items of rusty furniture. But I didn't expect to see someone lying in a pool of blood or meet a man who had spent the previous night in a seizure. A nurse, had there been one, would have known how to stop it, but the man stopped it himself by entering a coma.

There were so few nurses that patient care—feeding, washing and alerting the doctors in emergencies—was all done by family members. Mulago was a public hospital, and basic drugs and supplies should have been provided free, but they were rarely available. When a patient needed a drip line or an aspirin, a relative went to a market nearby. Nurses and doctors also sold equipment that in most cases had been stolen from the hospital stores. Doctors at Mulago earned four hundred dollars a year, nurses one hundred. It was not surprising to find them so alienated that they made what extra money they could from their patients. Many, having taken other jobs, didn't show up for work at all.

My friend went from bed to bed. There was another man in a coma, and another so weak he seemed able to move only his eyes. One patient had a private room. The place was tidy and sunny, and the sheets, unlike those in the public wards, were clean. He must have been rich. Someone had brought two straw shopping-bags full of provisions: cups and saucers, a Thermos flask, books, a soap dish. The patient looked all right to my untrained eye—not thin, no obvious rashes or sores, breathing quietly—except that he was moaning and writhing and holding his head. The doctor said he would give the man codeine, but that the only way to make him comfortable would be to knock him out completely. He died the next day anyway.

'Sometimes I don't know what I'm doing here,' the doctor said. 'I guess I'm really just here to help these people.'

What funding agencies want and what patients need often fail to coincide. Medical research here can be profoundly frustrating for the doctors who conduct the studies. They are caught between the demands of their employers to come up with convincing survival curves and the demands of their patients for help of any kind. A high proportion give up and leave. But for some, Mulago is a rewarding place, recalling a time when doctors were closer to their patients than they are now. Medicine in the West relies on expensive diagnostic techniques unavailable here; many doctors I spoke to in Uganda admit that they have learned a great deal from being forced to rely on a stethoscope. As one told me, 'I never realized there was so much you could learn just from listening to someone's heart.'

I withdrew after a while to sit on a wooden bench beside a thin, old man who was staring straight ahead and wheezing.

Between patients the doctor came over to me.

'Are you all right?' he asked. A funny question, I thought, to ask of someone visiting an Aids ward.

'I'm not sure I can take this.'

'I can understand that.'

I felt like a tourist, but without the contents of those boxes I was stuck and couldn't work. I tried to think of ways around it, of what local substitutions I could make, of what I could borrow from other scientists around Kampala. But what I was trying to do—design an HIV vaccine for Uganda—was way out on the high-tech edge. Many of the materials I needed had been designed in highly specialized laboratories in the United States. They existed in small quantities and were made nowhere else. To obtain them I had appealed to the generosity of these scientists, and they had responded. I didn't want to let them down.

3

The vaccines that protect people from infections are usually harmless fragments of the infection itself, often a virus or bacterium, introduced into the body in an injection or a pill. The body responds to this fragment as though it were the real thing and makes antibodies that remain in the blood for years and destroy the infection if it ever recurs. In the sixties, scientists discovered what antibodies looked like, and this told them a great deal about how they kill infections. Antibodies are Y-shaped molecules. At the ends of the arms of the Y, there are pockets, shaped like mittens, which can grab things. When an antibody grabs something, it signals to the other cells of the immune system to destroy it. The mittens are rigid, however, so once an antibody is made in response to an infection, or to a vaccine for that matter, it only works against that particular thing; if a different infection occurs, new antibodies must be made.

The difficulty in designing an HIV vaccine is suggested by what happens when the body responds to an HIV infection. A few weeks after becoming infected, many people become feverish, but this passes: the first antibodies to HIV have been made and they kill most of the virus particles. But some viruses escape by mutating: they change slightly so that they can no longer be grabbed by the antibodies. The body has to make new antibodies for the new mutant viruses, but the mutants then mutate more and escape again.

Over time, HIV goes on to kill the cells that control the production of antibodies (these are called T-cells), and the body's ability to chase the virus by making new antibodies is progressively weakened. In fact the body loses its ability to respond to any infection. Diseases of various kinds take over, and the patient slowly rots alive.

When I was preparing to come to Uganda, I learned that there were about thirty HIV vaccines being tested in the United States, but most Aids scientists had little hope that any vaccine would ever work because of the vast number of mutants. There are only two species of HIV (HIV-1 and HIV-2) but there are thought to be thousands, even millions, of mutants circulating in infected people around the world. Any effective vaccine must generate immunity to most, if not all, of them.

By all accounts, the most promising vaccine was the one designed in the lab of Dr Kathy Steimer of Chiron Corporation. It was her lecture at the university which, in its intelligence and pragmatism, had provided such relief from the tedious complexities of the insect entrails I was studying at the time. Shortly after Professor Cornelius said that I might be granted access to a bank of serum samples in Uganda, I went to see Dr Steimer at her lab at Chiron.

Chiron was founded in the late seventies by Professor William Rutter, the former chairman of the biochemistry department at the University of California, San Francisco. Members of his department had been the first to isolate a human gene and make copies of it in a test-tube, using a process called cloning. The gene made the hormone insulin, and cloning it permitted the large scale production of human insulin in the laboratory. It was hoped that this would help diabetics, who are unable to manufacture the hormone themselves.

Cloning provided an entirely new method for making drugs

and vaccines, and it immediately inspired visions of corporate empires in biology, similar to the computer empires that had been built a decade before, with biologists engineering drugs and vaccines for every human need.

Chiron now occupies a ten-acre lakeside compound near San Francisco, and employs two thousand people, paid for largely by the multi-billion-dollar sales of a vaccine for hepatitis B, the first cloned vaccine.

I recognized Dr Steimer immediately. She was tall and slim, with grey-blonde hair the colour of hay. She showed me around her lab: the two main rooms where work with uninfected specimens took place, and the isolation room for working with the live virus. To enter this room you had to wear a plastic body suit, two pairs of rubber gloves, a face mask, a hair net, unbreakable safety goggles and a pair of paper booties. I wondered if all that were necessary. Was the virus that dangerous to work with?

Dr Steimer explained that, although HIV mutates, she and her colleagues had a strategy that might contain it. At that time about five hundred HIV mutants had been identified. What was striking was that they seemed to fall into eight different categories known as subtypes, and these tended to circulate in specific populations around the world. Most people in the United States were infected with only one kind, subtype B. Dr Steimer's vaccine contained a single protein from the surface of the subtype-B virus. If the vaccine worked, it would protect people from infection by subtype B, but it was unlikely to protect people from the other subtypes circulating elsewhere in the world. Nevertheless, a vaccine for subtype B would be an enormous breakthrough. Because the vaccine was produced artificially by cloning, it contained none of the virus's genetic material and posed no risk of HIV infection.

A test of any vaccine proceeds in three phases. First it is administered to a small number of terminally-ill people to ensure that it does not accelerate their death. Next, it is given to a group of uninfected, healthy individuals to see if it induces them to make antibodies. This second phase usually involves an experiment in which blood is drawn from the volunteers and mixed with a sample of virus; if good antibodies have been produced they will kill the virus.

Phase three is a massive, fantastically expensive venture involving thousands of uninfected volunteers who are given either the vaccine or a placebo. The rates of infection in the placebo group and the vaccinated group are compared over a period of several years, and the statistics tell whether the vaccine protects people.

While the volunteers for a phase-three trial are healthy, they are chosen because they run a high risk of becoming infected. In the case of HIV they might be young gay men or intravenous drug users. They must be told that the vaccine is experimental and might not work and that, in any case, they may have received nothing more than the placebo. They are warned to take every measure to protect themselves. The success of the trial depends upon the fact that a significant number of these people—because of bad luck, stupidity or carelessness—will put themselves at risk anyway.

Dr Steimer's vaccine was in the second stage of testing. It had been deemed safe, and the antibodies produced by healthy volunteers killed various laboratory mutants of HIV subtype B. Dr Steimer and her colleagues were cautiously optimistic. The lab strains of HIV consisted of a pure stock of virus that had been propagated in an incubator for years; viruses taken from patients were more diverse and complex, having adapted to survival in the body rather than a plastic flask. Dr Steimer was preparing to test the volunteers' antibodies on wild strains of HIV, taken from real people with real infections. If the experiment worked, she would proceed to phase three.

Chiron could not finance a phase-three trial of the vaccine itself, but the United States Congress, on the advice of the National Institutes of Health, was considering pitching in with twenty million dollars. More lab data were required first. That decision was expected sometime the following year.

My thoughts were these: the World Health Organization, sensitive to the fact that the poorest nations might be overlooked in the high-tech scramble for an Aids vaccine, had designated four countries—Thailand, Brazil, Rwanda and Uganda—as potential sites for vaccine trials. Dr Steimer's vaccine was too expensive to test in a country that couldn't afford it. Nevertheless, if her vaccine turned out to work, and if information could be obtained about the subtypes circulating in Uganda, the company might consider making and testing a vaccine there in the future. It seemed possible that the United Nations or the World Bank would get involved.

My contribution would be to discover which subtypes of HIV were prevalent in Uganda. It seemed reasonable to believe that I could get this information by working with the samples that had been gathered in Kampala. Some information was already available, but it was incomplete, and came from all over the continent.

The easiest way to identify a virus subtype is by examining the antibodies that the body has created in response to becoming infected (which will reveal, in turn, what has caused the infection).

In the course of any disease, affected organs communicate with each other via the blood, which carries packets of information, in the form of molecules such as hormones or antibodies. There are blood-borne molecules that indicate pregnancy, kidney failure, diabetes or the presence of various infections. By investigating the molecules in a sample of a person's blood, you can learn a great deal without having to examine the organs directly.

These molecular messengers can be detected using a test called an ELISA—an enzyme-linked immuno-sorbent assay. One of Dr Steimer's colleagues had designed an ELISA that distinguishes antibodies against various HIV subtypes. It could tell if someone had been infected with A, B, C or some other subtype. Dr Steimer proposed that I use this technique to investigate the antibodies in the Kampala serum samples.

She told me that I could work in her lab on the San Francisco vaccine project for a couple of months to earn money and learn the ELISA technique. During those months, the ELISA became routine, and I planned my trip to Africa carefully. Not knowing what to expect, I packed as though I would be setting up an ELISA on the moon: chemicals, pipettes, pencils, tape, scissors. These were the materials that were lost on their way to Kampala.

Dr Steimer was prepared to pay for the materials I would need to do the the experiment, but not for me. I would have to support myself. The doctors in Kampala were prepared to let me use the stored blood samples and give me space in a lab, but weren't going to pay me either. Nevertheless, I was happy. The project was very small, and, although it would turn out that others were thinking along the same lines, I felt this work was my own. Such a feeling of independence is rare in biology. The hour of the lone scientist following his imagination into the unlit corners of nature is passing. These are the days of the Human Genome Project, the biotech revolution, and the five-million-dollar grant. Whatever you might want to do, others have thought of it already and they have more money, more technicians, more pipettes, more frogs, more of whatever it takes than you do. So you join their lab and do what they say or forget it.

4

Still waiting for my boxes, I arranged to meet Dr Arthur Murray at the Cancer Institute. I had not yet seen the serum samples that were the occasion for my being in Africa, and he promised to show them to me. Confident that my boxes would turn up, I thought I would get started sorting the samples out.

The vials were in the freezer in the main lab. They had been collected over the past four years, subjected to a routine HIV test and stored with numbers but no names. Arthur carefully opened the upright freezer. There must have been a hundred plastic sandwich bags full of vials. He put his hand out to make sure they wouldn't fall on the floor. My heart sank.

'They're kind of a mess,' he said.

They certainly were a mess. The vials were stored randomly, without regard to the age of the patients, or where they came from, or whether they were infected with HIV, or any detail of their medical history.

Arthur left me to sort through the samples, and I retreated to my salmon-coloured lab with a few soggy bags each containing about two hundred vials. It took an hour to sort through the first bag, from which I retrieved four samples that I thought I could use. The next bag went more quickly but it contained only three useable samples. By the end of the week, exhausted from boredom, I had 193. I decided to test these first and if my results were ambiguous in any way, I would somehow find the strength to return to the freezer for more.

But I needed my chemicals from San Francisco, and they still hadn't arrived.

So I had some time.

One day, I took a taxi across town to visit a friend, and the driver asked me what I was doing in Uganda. When I told him he bristled. 'How can you make a vaccine when the virus mutates so much? As soon as you make your vaccine, the virus turns into something else, and your old vaccine is useless.' I explained about neutralization and T-cell binding sites, and he seemed to accept this.

'So why bother looking at this V3 loop?' he asked.

'Well, we think that's important too . . .'

I had similar conversations with a construction worker, a group of high-school students, a hairdresser and the man who mopped the floor of the lab. I had to confront questions about virus mutability and why some people didn't get infected even though they were at high risk. Nowhere else had I found people as inquisitive and well-informed.

In Kampala there were Aids clubs, meetings, conferences, marches, candle-lit vigils, benefit breakfasts, lunches and dinners, T-shirts, hats, banners, books and cartoons; there were movies, plays, songs, poems and dances about Aids.

When I told the cab driver that I was impressed by how much people in Uganda seemed to know about HIV, he said, 'Everyone is affected by it. Everyone has a friend, a sister, someone who is sick or dead of Aids.'

Over the next year, I would hear over and over again that someone I knew had died or was burying a relative. Ugandans are used to seeing children die; for some, the death of a child is the only kind of death considered natural. But death in one's twenties and thirties used to be relatively rare. Now in parts of the country, Aids had increased the death-rate among young adults five-fold.

According to the World Health Organization, forty million Africans may be infected with HIV by the year 2015, and it will kill them all. It is hard to imagine what this means. The number is equivalent to the combined populations of Uganda, Tanzania and Zaire. Is it possible that whole countries will disappear? And why has Aids swept through Africa with such thoroughness and speed, when a similar epidemic has so far failed to emerge in the West.

Some people attribute the African epidemic to extreme promiscuity or exotic blood rituals, but such explanations are unconvincing. Surveys in many African cities show that people here have more sexual partners than people in the West, but not that many more. And while rituals involving the repeated use of sharp, bloody instruments do occur in Uganda—female circumcision and scarification, for instance—they are not practised by those groups with the highest levels of HIV infection. Anal sex and other forms of sodomy are rare here—or at least they are not admitted to.

The reason for the African epidemic might lie not in the number of sexual partners people have, but in who those partners are: in Africa sex crosses social boundaries more frequently than in the West. It occurs between rich and poor, urban and rural, old and young. In the West, Aids mainly affects gay men, who tend to have sex only with other gay men, and intravenous drug users, who, through needle sharing and sex, also tend to spread the virus among themselves.

In addition, Ugandans are often sick with something: they may be malnourished or have some exotic tropical disease. There are textbooks three inches thick describing illnesses that occur only in the narrow band of the earth's surface spanning the equator. This background of sickness may lower a person's resistance to infection from HIV.

But above all else, the African epidemic might be explained by the prevalence of sexually-transmitted diseases, as Professor Cornelius had explained back in San Francisco. During the first decades of this century, twenty per cent of all diseases at Mengo, Kampala's first missionary hospital, were sexually transmitted, and the figure is roughly the same at Kampala's main hospitals today. Penicillin and other antibiotics are too expensive for most Ugandans. When people here notice genital lesions, they ignore them or go to a diviner or a herbalist. They either get over these early symptoms or die, but they continue to have sex until it becomes too painful.

CHIPS had been a pilot project, a single clinic for sexually-transmitted diseases in a single urban slum. Similar clinics were planned for the rest of the country, but this was the first of its kind in Uganda.

We were on our way into town one day when Celeste told me that she intended to close CHIPS. She was going to the travel agent to buy tickets to visit a game park. She told me that she was preparing a flyer to distribute to everyone working on the project sometime in the next week. It would say that work had not been proceeding on schedule, and that USAID had decided to withdraw its grant. One hundred and thirty-two Ugandans would lose their jobs. Kisenyi would lose its clinic, and its people would continue to go without treatment.

Celeste told me how the end had come about.

It had taken her nine months to set up the CHIPS clinic, to hire and train the doctors, nurses, counsellors, drivers, accountants, statisticians and data-entry clerks. During this time a building had been renovated in Kisenyi, and enormous amounts of equipment and supplies had been purchased from the United States, shipped by air freight to Uganda and stored under lock and key at the Cancer Institute. Then Celeste left the country. She went to the Seychelles for a holiday, then to an Aids conference and on a speaking tour of the United States. She applied for, and was offered, a new job on the medical faculty of a prestigious Midwestern university. She returned to Uganda three months later.

On her return, she found that the odometer on the CHIPS vehicle had advanced by hundreds of miles, that money had disappeared from CHIPS bank accounts, and that a Ugandan colleague had put three of his sons on the payroll. Only thirty people had been treated at the clinic.

Clearly the project wasn't working, and yet from what Celeste told me, it should have been possible to make it work. Why did she give up? Was it really that she lost faith in her Ugandan colleagues? None of their crimes seemed so terrible. Or had she just lost interest in the project? I still don't know.

The day CHIPS closed I was out of town, visiting medical projects in western Uganda. Aids is considered less of a problem here, because there are fewer cases and because other diseases overwhelm it.

I went with a doctor friend to the district of Kabarole, about two hundred miles west of Kampala, in the foothills of the Rwenzori mountains where tea is grown on enormous, rolling plantations. We stopped in a village where tea workers lived in a row of huts made of reeds and mud. About twenty patients had assembled. We met the children first. They wore ragged American T-shirts and peered at us from around trees. When I smiled back and tried to take a picture, the older ones scattered, laughing, and hid behind the buildings; the little ones burst into tears.

We walked to a small building site where a school was under construction. A local doctor led us to an enclosure, 'our new clinic,' he joked, and the patients were asked to come in one by one. The first ones all had onchocerciasis—river blindness—a parasitic disease affecting the skin and eyes, endemic in the tropics. Outside in the tea fields all day, the patients had been bitten by the blackfly that transmits the disease. They had lumps under their skin, which contained coiled worms a foot long. Inside, the worms mated and reproduced, and their tiny offspring swam through the flesh, making it wrinkle and itch. I touched one of the lumps and could feel it move.

When the villagers learn that doctors are coming to town, they turn up with all kinds of complaints. There was a woman with an abscess, another with arthritis and a child with a fever. A teenager came in: she was shy, and, smiling, said something softly to our guide. He turned her by her shoulders so that her back was facing us, and undid her dress from the front. Her back was covered with tiny sores, some of them bleeding. 'This is not onchocerciasis,' our guide said. 'I think she suspects what it is.' This rash, I would learn, was an early indicator of HIV infection.

There were clinics like this all over rural Uganda. Many had no buildings or drugs, and consisted of a nurse or doctor who showed up only occasionally.

Some time later, I met a planner from the Ministry of Health who told me that the problem was not that the buildings were falling apart: a one-walled clinic is neither unusual nor impossible to work with. What were needed were drugs and decent salaries for health workers. 'With committed staff you can set up a clinic under a mango tree,' he said. I thought of USAID and its grand aim to control Aids with fancy clinics and condoms. I thought of CHIPS: $1.5 million, nearly one-tenth of Uganda's entire health budget, spent on a single clinic for sexually-transmitted diseases. I wondered whether money for salaries and cheap drugs for malaria and bacterial infections, including those that cause sexually-transmitted diseases, might not go a long way in controlling HIV, at least in those parts of Uganda where it was still relatively rare.

When I got back to Kampala, the CHIPS offices were cheerless. A few people were hanging around the administration building. Some were told they could work until the end of the month, others a little longer. Perhaps because it was an Aids project, CHIPS had been infused with an extraordinary enthusiasm; its employees believed in what they were working on. Now the spirit had drained out of them. Because I was white, I was asked by a few people to help them find new jobs, but what could I do?

That evening Celeste was remote. She said she had detected veiled personal threats. She had been warned, menacingly she thought, that it was dangerous to go out in Kampala at night. Alienation had settled in like a spell. She went away on safari to Kenya. During her absence, her cat and dog were mysteriously poisoned and died.

Before she left, Professor Cornelius, Celeste's boss, came out to Uganda. He arrived on the dawn flight from London and stayed at Celeste's house for a week. When I got up, he was sitting on the sofa, talking to a group of doctors. He spoke about a recent Aids meeting in Washington, about the business-class lounge at the airport, about who had been elected to the American College of Physicians (and who hadn't), the usual professional gossip.

During his visit, he met the Ugandan doctors at the Cancer Institute and learned how his work there was going—the professor was overseeing many projects. In addition to being in charge of a university department, he was the editor of a prestigious medical journal and he had also been appointed the private physician to an Arab sheikh. The professor lamented the closure of CHIPS, but said very little about it. One evening, he accompanied some of us to a local expatriate hangout in Kampala where prostitutes swanned up and put their hands in his pockets.

The professor was a little surprised to see me in Kampala. In fact everyone, including Celeste, wondered what I was doing here. Unlike them, I wasn't part of any institution. I wasn't part of CHIPS, or any of the other projects the professor was involved in, nor was I really part of Chiron, back in California. I was here simply because I had managed to interest Dr Steimer in the professor's serum samples. Perhaps because I had no clear identity, I was able to stow away on board their vessel. I lived in their houses and rode in their four-wheel-drive cars and listened to them talk about Aids; I prevailed on their generosity and on their hope that, if my project worked, and if, back in California, Chiron's vaccine turned out to work as well, a vaccine trial might be based here in the future. Then there would be a lot of work for them and for me. But for the time being, I was a hitch-hiker, and as hitch-hikers sometimes do, I became a little arrogant. Hitch-hikers live faithless, parasitic existences, but sometimes they see the landscape more clearly than the drivers.

During the professor's visit, he threw a party at the lab; many people came, including a European who had spent twelve years at an up-country hospital. He told me that, during the civil war, parties would last all night because it was too dangerous to go home. The shooting started at about four in the afternoon, and wherever you were then, there you would stay until morning. He and his Ugandan colleagues were on their own in those days. They had few drugs and almost no supplies; sometimes it was impossible to find clean water to wash out gunshot wounds. Things were much easier now.

Our group of Americans looked up to this man, but I don't know how he felt about us. He told us, perhaps only partly in jest, that they talk about two kinds of Aids in Uganda: slim Aids and fat Aids. People with slim Aids get thinner and thinner and thinner until they finally waste away. Fat Aids afflicts doctors and bureaucrats who get enormous research grants and fly around the world to exotic places and get fatter and fatter and fatter. Fat Aids has become so common in Uganda, he told us, that if you say you are working on HIV people think you are a thief.

5

A curious thing happened a few days after CHIPS was cancelled. My boxes turned up. They were locked in the storeroom, and had been there a month. After the project closed, Celeste handed the keys to the storeroom back to USAID—all the equipment and drugs kept there were due to be returned. I knew that my materials would be there. It was the only place I hadn't looked.

Celeste should have known where the boxes were; she had been the only one with the key. But she had been distracted and upset and perhaps she overlooked or ignored them. The day I found the boxes I ran into her on the path at the Cancer Institute.

'Oh! You found everything! Great!' She smiled and moved on quickly.

Some of the Ugandans should have known about the boxes too, because they would have put them there. The chief accountant kept track, or was supposed to, of everything that came and went from the Institute. I remember describing the boxes to him in great detail and presenting him with a list of their contents. He gave me a big smile and promised he would search. I checked back every day. Had he seen them? No, not yet, but they were sure to turn up soon.

And yet there they were. Whomever I chose to complain to would blame it on someone else, or just smile.

By now, I had detected in the way people phrased things that there was a vague, but consistent, confusion between accident and responsibility. If something fell or broke, Ugandans said, 'Sorry!' At first, I was tempted to reply, 'That's OK, it's not your fault,' but I soon realized that they knew it wasn't. When someone crashed his car, he said, 'The car got an accident,' like catching a cold. Caught stealing a cassette tape, the gardener said, 'It just got in my pocket.'

This is what physicists call Brownian motion, the random

movement of particles, on a grand scale. The natural world is statistical. When you turn on the tap, the most likely outcome is that water will flow from the tank on the roof into the sink. But there is a very small probability, immeasurable or nearly so, that all the molecules will drift the other way. Here I have seen the margins of probability widen considerably. Water still flows downhill in general, but the wily gardener may have turned off the supply. He'll blame it on the old pipes the stingy landlord put in and request 'money to pay the plumber' to fix them. Disorder is driven by a tide so strong it pulls everything with it, and the careless, dishonest and greedy coast through the current with ease.

I built and dismantled various paranoid scenarios. Perhaps they had something against vaccine projects. This would not be a trivial matter. In the early eighties a medical relief worker was vaccinating people against polio on the Ssese Islands in Lake Victoria. Both he and his vaccine were unpopular for reasons I do not know, and the islanders allegedly rowed him out in a canoe to a place where the lake was deep, tied a rock around his neck and threw him overboard.

Maybe the storekeepers didn't like me; maybe they didn't like Celeste; maybe they didn't like me because I lived with Celeste. Shortly I became too busy to worry about it.

After Celeste left, I moved to a house on Makindye Hill, technically part of the city of Kampala, but very rural. On the way to my new house, I would walk up a red dirt road, dispersing clouds of butterflies. Small plots of cassava and banana had been cut out of the bush. Goats and chickens grazed on the verges. A troop of green monkeys swung in the trees outside my window, and one morning I woke up early and saw a wild grey parrot take off from his perch on a bush. I shared a room with an assortment of insects: ants, grasshoppers, millipedes and a shoehorn-sized flying beetle in need of pilot lessons. It tripped over things on the floor, bumped into walls, and made a sound like a small helicopter with its wings. I watched it during a case of insomnia brought on by the anti-malaria pills I was taking. The problem seemed to be that when it landed it fell over on its side and then had to buzz its wings to right itself. How could such a species endure? I have come to believe that almost anything can survive in this climate. There is only variation and no selection, so life pours out of here as from a volcano. It is the only place on earth where a feeble, unsteady, slow-moving, hairless species such as man could have evolved.

Small perturbations of the environment cause extreme changes. Organisms bloom and disappear. New species turn up. Patients returning from Africa with diarrhoea, rashes and fevers often undergo every lab test at the Hospital for Tropical Diseases in London, but cannot be diagnosed. Most of these illnesses go away. HIV may just be a rare invention of nature that's here to stay for a while.

Where did it begin? Uganda is sometimes credited with being the place where Aids originated, but this may simply be because it was the first African country to open its borders to Aids research: other countries, with lucrative tourist industries to protect, were less open at first; Uganda, recovering from civil war, had little to lose and much to gain by inviting the West to come and study its diseases. I don't know whether HIV came from Uganda, but I think it is safe, both historically and diplomatically, to say that HIV originated somewhere in Africa.

Some German medical students on a tour of Uganda told me that they had heard of a British doctor in the forties, working in what was then the Congo, who described cases of a mysterious wasting disease. His African patients associated it with adulterous behaviour. The doctor's observations were said to have been published in the *Lancet*, but I haven't found the article. This was probably another one of the rumours one hears all the time. Nevertheless it is possible that the first cases of the disease occurred here.

One species of the virus, known as HIV-2, almost certainly crossed into human populations from the sooty mangabey, a West African monkey. This monkey carries a virus very similar to HIV-2. It is not unprecedented in the history of infectious disease for people to become infected with animal viruses. Measles probably originated in dogs, and they still carry it although it doesn't make them ill. Flu can be deadly to humans, but is harmless to pigs, and it is thought that Chinese pigs are the incubators for new flu strains. Upon moving into a new, unadapted host-species, parasites sometimes become unlicensed and virulent. Eventually a successful parasite must learn by evolution not to kill its host, because in killing it, it destroys itself too. But the relationship takes time to settle down. What we have in the meantime is disease.

What act permitted HIV-2 to cross the species boundary from monkeys to people is not known. It might have been killing and eating the monkeys, fresh blood on an injured hand, or something more exotic: interspecies sex or transfusions of monkey blood as an aphrodisiac. Beyond the molecular similarity between HIV-2 and the monkey virus, it is probably impossible to know more.

I opened my boxes. Everything was there: the plastic jars containing powdered chemicals, bottles, aluminium foil, waterproof pens, a roll of pink tape. I had also packed three micropipettes, pistol-sized instruments capable of measuring one millionth of a litre of fluid. These were the most expensive items of all, costing about $150 each—a gift from a friend at Chiron whose social conscience had been stirred when I gave a short talk about the work I planned to do in Uganda.

My primary concern now was water. The water from the taps (when there was water from the taps) came from Lake Victoria and sometimes was a faint brown colour and had things floating in it—not the best medium in which to observe controlled molecular reactions. To do my experiments, I needed distilled water. The Cancer Institute functioned without distilled water, because the experiments conducted there used pre-packed kits shipped at great expense from the United States.

In town there was a medical research lab run by the government, which had shrewdly recognized that its country's diseases might constitute a kind of non-traditional export. The lab functioned on a for-hire basis; for a price, scientists from anywhere in the world could come here to study the sick in Uganda. This lab had, I was told, the finest water in the country.

The lab was in a long, white building with a well-kept lawn meticulously cut with machetes, and was guarded by soldiers in camouflage uniforms. I went to visit, but the director was not in.

I asked his deputy if I could inspect his water and use it for my experiments. He told me that if I wanted water, I should write a proposal. I needed to state who I was, what my project was and what I wanted the water for.

OK, that's what they do here, I figured, and drafted a two-paragraph letter. I asked the secretary at the Cancer Institute to type it and forward a copy to the head of the Cancer Institute. Upon reading the letter, the head of the Cancer Institute decided that it would be better if the letter came from him as he was senior to me and therefore in a better position to negotiate. Eventually, a letter, written by me, typed by the secretary and signed by the director made its way to the government lab. After a week, I had heard nothing, so I went to find the director again. This time he was in. He had lost the letter. I explained everything again. He said, yes, I could use his water.

The government lab was immaculate and vast, staffed by seven technicians all wearing lab coats, ties and clean, white sneakers. Some were setting up cultures to diagnose tuberculosis; others were measuring out samples of a herbal mixture, which, it was claimed, relieved the nausea and diarrhoea associated with Aids. It had the consistency of alfalfa, but no one could tell me what it was.

I met one young lab assistant whose only assignment seemed to be to watch water drip out of the still. He was small and stooped and limped a little when he walked. He sat for hours on a white counter-top and stared at the still with a cheerful, lazy smile. At lunchtime, he removed his lab coat and turned off the machine. As he headed for the door, I asked him to turn it back on.

'Don't worry,' I said, 'I'll watch it.' I then went back to calculating how much sodium hydroxide I would need to adjust the pH of borate to nine.

When I looked up again, grey steam was pouring out of the still. Apparently the water supply had been cut off, and the machine's bare coil was red hot. A two-thousand-dollar piece of equipment, unavailable in Uganda, had almost been ruined. The technicians were forgiving. They said it had happened before; the still could be fixed.

The demons of accident are a feature of scientific work, and the thoughts of most scientists, when they are not taken up by revolutionary perceptions of nature and disease, are mainly concerned with preventing things from screwing up. But I was used to problems on a smaller scale: a bad batch of some chemical, dirty pipettes, bacteria growing where they shouldn't be, stray bits of fluff from the air, careless little mistakes. In Uganda accidents were of an entirely different order.

At the end of the week I returned to my own lab with a dozen bottles of solutions and started the ELISA tests. After the refrigerator had been installed, there was no room for me, so I had to work in the main lab after all. The place was crowded; six of us in a very small space. Nurses came and went delivering specimens from the hospital, vials of urine and blood and other things to be tested for pregnancy, diabetes, syphilis, HIV infection. Sometimes the nurses hung around chatting. Sometimes a person I didn't know would sit near my little corner, blocking my only way out, and spread thousands of tiny pieces of paper everywhere. The other technicians were very big, and we all tried to avoid sudden movements.

I ran through the ELISA as I had learned it at Chiron, adapting the procedure slightly to this African lab. It was a pleasure and a relief to see the read-out of the first experiment. An array of green dots appeared on a plastic dish, each one corresponding to a single patient and a single HIV subtype. The greener the dot, the more antibodies the person had made in response to that subtype, and the more likely he was to have been infected with it.

In experiments of this kind, in which many samples are subjected to the same test, it is important to create a routine so that everything is done as neatly and quickly as possible. All actions are economized and simplified. The aim is to design a procedure that can be followed without thinking.

On the first day, I processed four patients' samples. All were infected with HIV-1, but they carried different subtypes. One had antibodies against subtype A, and another had antibodies against subtype B. Two turned out to have antibodies against both subtypes A and D.

The next day I processed four more samples. These patients had antibodies against B only, D only, both A and B, and nothing.

The routine was pleasant and not yet boring, and I discovered little tricks to make things go more smoothly. It would be some time before the implications of what I was finding sank in.

I was intrigued by the diversity of antibody types that turned up in these experiments. The results were very different from what I had seen in California. Everybody there had antibodies to subtype B. It was hard to identify any trend in the way the Ugandan samples behaved.

After three weeks, I had tested about fifty samples. I sent a page of data to Chiron to let them know that work was underway. I said I thought the results were interesting and wondered if they did too. I spoke to a post-doc in Dr Steimer's lab, and he said he was pleased that the experiment was working. He told me to keep going.

One morning I arrived to find the lab dark. The chief technician sat by the window, reading a newspaper. Two other technicians, one a sceptic, the other a Catholic, were arguing about the Ten Commandments. The Cancer Institute has a back-up generator, but it had burnt out from overuse. The hospital engineer had been by, but he only looked at the generator and shook his head. The administrator went to call the electricity company. The phone was out of order. We drove to the electricity company, found the manager and told him that we were doing Aids research at Mulago; that our work was being ruined; that lives were at stake; that he had to do something.

The problem was with the transformer, he said. There was nothing he could do. He wouldn't even accept a bribe.

Was anyone working on it?

No. The engineers were busy elsewhere.

We went back to the lab, and the lights were, miraculously, on, but it was too late to start an experiment.

That night the transformer at the hospital exploded in a flash that lit up the sky over half the city. A friend watched it burn from a balcony café in town. Then the hill where the hospital was went dark. My friend called me. 'Don't bother coming to work,' she said, 'for a week, at least.' She was being pessimistic. A few days later the lights were on again.

As the weeks wore on, more problems occurred; although they were always unpredicted, the novelty soon faded. Sometimes I wondered if I shouldn't have stayed in the United States, where boxes don't disappear, refrigerators don't shrink, water flows on demand, and labs rarely blow up. But Aids research in the United States would have meant a contract, a salary and a boss. The boss would have told me that what I was trying to do wasn't worth it; the vaccine would fail, and Ugandans wouldn't be able to afford it anyway. But mine was a romantic, naïve, ill-conceived mission that just might work, and, for that reason, the struggles were never too hard to endure. It would have been much harder to do something I didn't believe in.

Perhaps, I thought, CHIPS collapsed because it belonged to no one. When it got into trouble, USAID didn't care, because, in the jargon typical of the profession, its role is planning, not implementation; it provides money and decides how it should be spent, but gets someone else to do the work. The Africans didn't care, because they wanted doctors and medicine, not buildings and condoms and lectures about sex. And Dr Quinn had other plans.

While I was working on the ELISAs, the phlebotomist at the Cancer Institute died. Towards the end, I was told, he was so sick that he frightened the patients. He wore a scarf to hide his swollen neck. I asked the American technologist in charge of the lab if she thought many people who worked at the Cancer Institute were infected with HIV. 'You know that cute, little pregnant nurse who hangs around the ward?' she asked. I did. She was beautiful, small with perfect features like a child, and enormously pregnant. She was married to the phlebotomist.

After I had been in the lab for some time, I started helping a technician who was growing cells from HIV-infected patients in dishes in the incubator. There were indications that something was wrong. Some of the cells were dying, some of the time, but we couldn't predict when or figure out why; but most of the cells were OK and producing lots of virus particles, perhaps as many as a hundred every second.

I suggested to the technician that he test his cultures to see if they were too acidic or too alkaline. He put a drop of one culture on a piece of litmus paper. Impatient to know the answer, I grabbed the wet piece of paper with a bare hand. The pH was within acceptable limits. Then I realized what I had done: the solution was far more infectious than any bodily fluid, including blood. I washed my hands four times.

I did some research and discovered that there have been quite a few cases in which workers were infected on the job. Most involved an accident with a needle or a scalpel. But one doctor was infected when blood splashed on his chapped hand. A technician was infected when plasma splashed in her eye. Since 1978, there have been thirty-two cases of infection among lab workers where no other risk factor was present. In four, the technician could recall no incident other than percutaneous exposure. That is, it got through the skin somehow, through a small cut or maybe the edge of a fingernail.

How many lab workers with other risk factors had become infected on the job, but had been eliminated from the statistics? How did we know that the real lab infection rate wasn't higher?

I thought of all the careless mistakes I had made. Once I found that I had dropped acid in a wastepaper basket, and another time contaminated a test tube with radioactivity. On both occasions, I was the only one who could have done it, but even now I don't remember making those mistakes. How many times had I done this kind of thing? And how many times had it involved the Aids virus?

Over the next couple of weeks, a mild headache came and went. I felt tired. I had a fever, diarrhoea, an ear infection. I became aware of my neck and armpits.

Everyone in the health field worries about it. The American technologist told me that she tests herself every six months or so by ELISA—a test similar to the one I was using for the subtyping experiments. The read-out at the end of the test is also an array of dots, each corresponding to a different person. The dots tell you who is infected. If the dot is white, the person is uninfected; if the dot is green, the person is infected. One day, she looked at the test plate and, in the place where her own sample should be, she saw a green dot. She was infected. One of the technicians noticed that she had been staring at the plate for a long time. He looked over her shoulder. He told her that she was holding it upside down. She was not infected.

For months, I felt mildly ill. I knew I should have a test. The doctor I went to see told me she had been a surgeon in Africa for six years. She had done operations, deliveries, Caesareans. Forty per cent of the women attending the hospital were HIV positive. The doctor said she had cut herself, stuck herself with needles, been forced to work without gloves because the hospital was too poor to supply enough of them. She had not become infected. While I waited for the results, I went shopping. I took a long walk. The world had never looked so beautiful. I was not infected.

At the end of three months, I had data on almost two hundred patients, enough to convince myself that Ugandan HIV antibodies were a very mixed bag. Most patients had antibodies against subtypes A, B or D, but there were many people who had antibodies against more than one subtype: such as both A and B; or both A and D; or A, B and D. I saw almost every conceivable combination. Perhaps these people were infected with more than one virus in the first place. On the other hand, they may have been infected with different, *new* subtypes that merely shared characteristics of some of the known ones. Whatever the interpretation, the diversity of viruses here seemed to be very great.

I was not surprised. If the virus had originated in Africa, and had been here longer than anywhere else, you would expect to find a large number of subtypes. Perhaps for decades, even a century, HIV propagated through African populations. During this time, it mutated and evolved. More recently, perhaps in the sixties or seventies, one or a small number of infected people brought HIV to the West. Perhaps they brought subtype B. The first clusters of Aids cases in gay men in the United States occurred in the late seventies, after which subtype B fanned out all over the Americas and Europe. In the decades to come, American varieties may evolve in the same way and may be entirely new.

Interesting perhaps, but the practical implications were disturbing. My results showed that an HIV vaccine for Uganda would have to be designed differently from the subtype-B vaccine being tested in the United States. It would have to include a cocktail of many different HIV types. To make such a vaccine would take two or three years, at least, and cost millions of dollars to design and test.

I sent my results to Chiron by fax. I looked forward to discussing the implications of what I had found and learning how the trial of the subtype-B vaccine was going.

There was no reply for several days. Then there was a weekend, and then no reply for a few more days. I asked Arthur if he had any idea what might be going on.

'People forget about you over here. We're too far away. You just have to accept that what happens in Africa doesn't matter much back home.'

Finally I got a reply from Chiron. It was a letter from the post-doc I had spoken to before. He said that in order to draw any conclusions from the data I sent, more work would have to be done on the Ugandan serum samples. Would it be possible, he asked, for me to send some actual samples back to Chiron? If Chiron confirmed my results using other, more technically advanced methods, then perhaps we could write a paper about HIV antibodies in Uganda and their implications for vaccine design. This information would help anyone interested in working on a vaccine for Uganda, even if it were different from Chiron's.

As it happened, Arthur was preparing to go back to San Francisco to take up a medical fellowship. We spoke to the director of the Cancer Institute, and he agreed to allow him to take twenty-five vials of serum to Chiron.

I packed the samples the morning of the day Arthur left. He promised he would send them across San Francisco Bay to Chiron, a forty-minute trip by car, soon after he arrived. I was grateful for his help, with this and with everything else. It was thanks to him that this venture had worked at all. He had convinced the people who ran the lab to let me work there and had driven me around town in search of boxes and water. He had been working in Uganda as an epidemiologist for two years, counting people as they got sick and died; and he had become depressed by the failures of Uganda's dilapidated hospitals and its public health campaigns, which, though vigorous, were not very effective. He and I shared the hope that the answer to Aids in Uganda would emerge from an incubator in the West someday.

I stayed in Uganda after Arthur left and became involved in another Aids project here. But I never heard from Chiron or from Arthur. I went to England, but was drawn to return to Uganda.

During the next year, I followed the story of Chiron's vaccine in the pages of scientific journals. Further experiments showed that the Chiron subtype-B vaccine might protect people from lab mutants of the virus, but not from mutants currently circulating in infected people in the United States. Perhaps ten years ago, when the strains that are in the lab now were circulating in real people, the vaccine would have had a better chance, but now we are dealing with different viruses. We just can't keep up. It occurred to me that this was just what everyone had warned me about: the HIV researchers in the United States and even the cab driver in Kampala. This virus evolves faster than antibodies, and much faster than any vaccine. It turns every corner and eludes us.

By the time I left Uganda for the last time, in May 1994, a multi-million-dollar trial of the subtype-B vaccine was looking pretty ambitious. That June, a committee of Aids experts at the US National Institutes of Health decided they felt the same way. They unanimously rejected a proposal to finance a trial of the Chiron vaccine in the United States.

I also learned from the scientific literature that I was not the only one studying HIV subtypes in Africa. Others had been doing the same experiment in Zaire, Zimbabwe and the Central African Republic. Their results were similar to mine. All this information currently awaits the invention of a different kind of vaccine.

We may wait a long time. If science ever does solve Aids, the answer will almost certainly come from a direction in which most of us are not looking. Nothing we know about biology and medicine now seems to be of much use. We need another revolution, something such as cloning or the splitting of the atom.

Even then, Uganda probably won't benefit much. Most people here die of malaria, bacterial infections of the gut and respiratory tract, nutritional deficiencies and measles, all preventable or curable.

As Arthur was leaving, our parting words were these: 'So you're going to send those samples to Chiron?'

'I promise.'

'I'm counting on you. All you have to do is carry them across the bay.'

'I know. I will.'

Twelve months have elapsed, and the samples are still in a freezer in Arthur's department in San Francisco.

Everyone seems to think they know what Africa needs, but sometimes I think our minds are not really on it. Most of us see only Africa's contours, and we use them to map out problems of our own. Africa is a career move, an adventure, an experiment. It fades into an idea.

We aren't really looking. I think of the dot in the cells of the bug under the microscope in the lab back in California. Although the fine machinery of insect cells means less to me now, I did draw at least one lesson from that work: biology teaches you that if you look hard enough at a problem you will find something. But you have to look very hard. You must enter its world, and, as if in a trance, follow its logic and forget your own.

From the moment you are exposed to the HIV virus to when an infection can be detected with a test takes about three months. For three months, I lived with the possibility that I had Aids. Sometimes it seemed certain that I did. Every morning, on the way to the lab, I passed a clinic where HIV-positive patients lined up on benches on a porch waiting to see the doctor. He weighed them, took a blood sample and sent them home. Sometimes a man or woman had to be carried up the steps from the road, thin and weak with limbs swinging like a marionette's. I wondered how those who were not yet sick dealt with this. They said nothing and looked away. It is a lonely disease. You die slowly, in great pain, and everyone is frightened of you. I realize now that as I passed them, I could almost see across the distance of continents and race. Very briefly, I thought I saw Aids their way.

NURUDDIN FARAH
FALSE ACCOUNTING

I grew up in the Ogaden, a semi-arid province of the world's poorest empire, where the Ethiopian dollar was in such short supply that we used the East Africa shilling of the British colonies to the south-east. That we lived in an empire in rags and depended on the minting industries of a wealthier one outside our boundary proved to be a microcosm of our continent's future. Today, totally reliant on food grown elsewhere and on goods manufactured across the seas, a market woman in Africa calculates her income not in the Nigerian naira, the Zambian kwacha, the Moroccan dinar or the Kenyan shilling but in the American dollar. She dwells in an alienated economy not unlike the Ogaden of my childhood.

I knew about money and the injustices associated with it long before I was big enough to earn any of my own. My father owned a retail business, selling his merchandise at a profit to nomads who would come in the morning, wearing robes brown with the dust of travel, and set up their base for the day at our compound. At dusk, their business over, they left. On these day trips, they sold their goats, sheep and cattle to middlemen who charged them hefty commission, only to spend much of the money at my father's shop on items such as sugar, oil, soap and other necessities. Observing them with curiosity as they counted and recounted their money, I often wondered why they allowed others to take advantage of them, noticing how they tied the very little they had saved on to the edges of their robes, wary of pickpockets.

I spied on their comings and goings, ready to talk and listen to their stories whenever the opportunity came, and this was how I discovered that my father dealt with them unfairly, selling his wares to them at extortionate prices and buying theirs at a rate favourable to him.

For several years I earned my pocket money by writing letters in English or Arabic on behalf of men or women who did not know how to read or write. Aside from this being a source of income for a schoolboy, the stories they told me were fascinating, and I became privy to their adult worries and secrets, which I was honour-bound not to divulge. These men and women spoke their minds on matters of political, economical and cultural importance, affording my young mind access to the tribulations of the period before I reached my teens.

I learned more than other boys my age about the evil nature of money and the corruption of the world. Not yet ten and already a citizen of a number of kingdoms by virtue of my contacts with these men and women, I pleaded with my brother to explain what was happening in a language I could follow. It was then that I first heard the word 'colonialism', as part of a long-winded pontification on the subject of money. The phrase 'the colonized world's economic history' remains with me till this day, although I can't somehow disentangle it from the Gordian knot in which it is forever tied.

Thirty years on, living in Nigeria, I find myself re-visiting the conversations of my youth. Now, as I repeat my brother's words, it is my wife who asks why the idea of money is so problematic in today's Africa.

I answer that in pre-colonial Africa, alongside a variety of currencies, there was a traditional system of barter. This was undermined by colonialism, when Africa's commodity currency—the exchange rate of barter—was replaced with modern moneys. These were linked with Europe's economy; and all transactions, including the salaries of the expanding labour force, were paid in European coins.

What kind of currencies did Africa have before then?

'In the Ethiopian kingdom of Axum, for instance,' I reply, 'coins were in circulation in the third century. The coins boasted the kings' heads, with liturgical inscriptions on one side and the Christian cross on the other. Africans to the north of the Sahara were the first to monetize their regional economies and create urban centres, perhaps because of their proximity to Muslim societies. They based their currencies on gold or silver dinars.'

What of sub-Saharan Africa?

'Exchanges were effected either by barter,' I say, 'or through other intermediary currencies: the "banknotes" were bands of cotton cloth, the "coins" cowries or other sea shells. In some areas, gold was exchanged for its weight. Taxes and tributes were paid partly in currencies, partly in provisions supplemented by symbolic gifts, such as a leopard's or a lion's skin. A hunter bartered game in exchange for iron.'

My wife laments that we live in a world stood on its head—

all important international deals are made in the currencies of the wealthiest countries. What do I think the lasting influences of the introduction of a money economy have been?

'For a start,' I say, 'Africa's economic progress was arrested by devaluing its traditional barter system. A new standard of wealth was imposed, based not on the sheep, cattle or camels one owned but on cash. What's more, people no longer worked for subsistence and the good of their community, but in order to earn money. This led to the establishment of a class of wage-earners and a salaried workforce.'

I explain that the banking activities which accompanied the colonial money economy were part of the process that integrated Africa into a world economy from which it did not benefit.

'In fact,' I argue, 'Africa's inability to adjust to current economic trends may be traced to these imbalances. No continent can recover from relentless imperialist expansion: being invaded and looted and having its able-bodied, skilled manpower taken away and enslaved. All this put paid to Africa's hope of development.'

Money is an item of foreign manufacture. All natives love it!

As an inheritor of a new standard of wealth based on cash, I am conscious of my precarious place in a continent where there is a great deal of poverty, and where most people are convinced that those with links to Europe have more money than they do.

For these reasons, my wife and I hesitated before buying a second-hand Mercedes imported to Nigeria from Belgium. Mercs are but symbols of status. Furthermore, to most Nigerians my wife and I are 'alien'—of the not-native-to-these-parts variety: she is Nigerian on her father's side but English on her mother's, and I am a Somali. In the same way that people assume we are foreign, they tend to deduce that we are affluent.

As I watch a stream of men and women walk past the window of my study in Kaduna, I assume they think of wealth as a foreigner living in a mansion, while the native dwells in poverty, cramped in a hovel, twelve to a room. My wife, my daughter and I live in a three-bedroom bungalow, whereas just across the fence from our garden, the world takes a poorer aspect. I imagine the envious thoughts astir in our neighbours' minds as

175

they stare at me, reading or writing. Probably they think, 'Money'. In today's Africa, foreigners, politicians, uniformed men or dishonest businessmen are moneyed.

Although our house is modest, we have had to beef up its security in the sick knowledge that because we are perceived to be rich foreigners we may fall victim to the murderous conspiracies hatched in the heads of armed robbers. Eight-o'clock-in-the-morning break-ins are commonplace in Kaduna, as are night-time burglaries involving a dozen men armed with machine-guns, masked gangsters prepared to kill or maim to get what they are after. 'In these hard times,' my wife says, 'a couple presumed to be Oyibo—you an Arab-looking man with a half-caste wife, driving a Mercedes—will definitely attract the attention of the dispossessed.'

We have taken prophylactic measures to protect ourselves from possible attacks, building a kind of metal barricade to our sleeping area and leaving a couple of electric gadgets in the living-room, offerings in case they break in.

Will the robbers fall for our bait? Will they bargain with us?

Bargaining is an art form in some cultures. For me the process becomes not only a bid to alter the asking price to my advantage but also a means of making personal contact. On occasion, Somalia, the high watermark of my exiled state, comes under discussion as I haggle with a salesman in Kaduna. Instantly friendlier now that he can place me somewhere in Africa, the seller speaks with deep sympathy about Somalia's tragedy, never failing to conclude, 'We hope Nigeria won't be like your country.' All the same I feel triumphant if I knock a digit or two off the asking price. The Hausaman who comes to our house once a week with neatly-wrapped vegetables on the saddle of his bicycle insists that I listen to his stories in exchange for any discount he might give.

My wife, who does not associate bargaining with any kind of gratification, asks, 'Why do you bother? It is such small change. Let them have it.'

Tongue in cheek, I point out the pleasures of adept bargaining, with the buyer and the seller sizing each other up, both putting in a good wrestle in an effort to floor the other with a counter-argument.

She quotes a maxim, "'Who has money spends it; who doesn't, talks about it." How much do you save? It's all a pittance, I would say, not worth the bother.'

Our Igbo-speaking carpenter shares the widely-held opinion that we are rich. He refuses to believe that I cannot afford to pay for wall-to-wall panelling in imported teak. Nothing I say or do will change his view. Thinking I am just mean, he mumbles to himself that it is all part of a moneyed man's posturing, 'What's this—"we have no money"?' He pauses, adding, as though he were in secret communication with our bank manager, 'But you get plenty of money!' We were in full swing, bargaining, minting not money but words!

Time is not money in Africa, where words are accorded a higher value than in Europe. I am reminded of an afternoon when my mother called on me to persuade me to offer some money to a poorer relation. Since I knew what she had come for, I cut her short by suggesting that she take my wallet and help herself to as much money as she pleased. But my mother protested. Only beggars, she said, were offered alms on the basis of a standard formula, which they recited again and again. She had come with sorrowful words of someone else's tongue, and I had better listen to her.

In my day I have known salesmen to be put out by a buyer having the money to pay for the item in question but not the words with which to grease the gears of human communication. And I myself hadn't the patience to lend rhythm to the sorrow of my mother asking for money on behalf of a relation struck with misfortune.

There is a folk-tale about a poor man who has a rich man for his neighbour. The rich man, suffering from insomnia, attributes it to his worries about wealth and how to make more of it, or how not to lose it or be dispossessed of it. Then one day he lights on a generous idea, that of giving away half his wealth to his penniless neighbour, whom he knows to be at peace with his own mind and who sleeps like a baby. Asked why he parted with half his wealth, the rich man replies that by giving away so much, he hopes he will buy peace of mind. Which he does. And he, too, then sleeps like a baby.

177

The poor man, on the other hand, sleeps less and less; he is awake until the small hours, then up again at dawn, looking after the wealth with which he has been entrusted, certain that it won't take care of itself. No longer a poor man and no longer closeted away in his impoverished cubicle of inner tranquillity, he finds it difficult to relax. Six months go by and, realizing that his insomnia is the result of his current worries, he returns the wealth and the preoccupations that come with it to their lawful owner. Only then does peace reign in his mind.

To this story my wife responds, 'I am not sure that rich people worry about money more than poor people do. I find in fact, the people who worry most about money are those living in a country where the local currency is completely unstable. It has nothing to do with being poor or rich.'

Nodding in agreement, I observe that in Nigeria, people have started to talk obsessively about money ever since the recent devaluation of the naira. In their plaintive mood, people curse the government and bad-mouth the now-big men who were paupers only a couple of years earlier, the upstarts who display their ill-gotten wealth in the most blatant manner.

A few days after our arrival in Kaduna, my wife drove me round in a borrowed car, pointing out the mansions and telling me who owns them, and where these owners might have obtained their corrupt money, supplying me with evidence that would rarely be accepted in court. Friends have driven me round Nairobi, Abidjan, Banjul, their fingers pointing out the government as the nerve centre of corruption. Drinking in bars, or sitting at dinner, or just talking, people entertain one another with tales that sound taller than the highest sky-scraper: and yet most of them are true!

My wife comments, 'Only stolen wealth is spent so obscenely!'

'Like drugs money?' I ask.

'Precisely,' she agrees. 'After all no drugs baron worth a pinch of his cocaine will keep his money in cash in his house or on his person. He can never relax and enjoy his wealth.'

Meandering, our conversation leads us to roads paved with generalizations about wealth and Africa. I hypothesize that here you can easily tell rich countries from poor ones not by the statistics in almanacs, but by the number of foreigners living there and the sort of lifestyle they enjoy. In the rich countries, you find the type who stay in expensive foreign-currency hotels and are chauffeur-driven to meetings where they sit opposite government ministers in air-conditioned offices, laid with oriental carpets. Later in the day they are taken for a photo session with the head of state. In poor countries, you find the foreigners who are driven in Jeeps or Land-Rovers bearing insignias of aid organizations, men and women as rugged-looking as their stone-washed jeans, their hair unkempt, beards unshaven, their toe-nails uncut. Every so often you come across a clutch of evangelists converting malnourished Africans to alien faiths. The expensively-attired work for multinationals, the United Nations or inter-governmental bureaucracies; the poorly clad are employed by non-governmental agencies, and their business masquerades as charity.

My wife observes, 'Nowadays there are fewer foreigners of either category in Nigeria. In the oil-boom days when the naira was exchanged as if on a par with the dollar, you had legions of tight-lipped Europeans and Americans in business suits, filling hotel bars and doing deals with loudly-laughing Nigerian counterparts. And Nigeria doesn't yet attract the aid organizations, because it is apparently considered too wealthy to qualify for their benevolence.'

I travel a great deal, changing countries, continents and currencies frequently enough to confirm my no-belonging status.

In any given year, I deal with a medley of moneys, not to mention exchange rates—some above board, some under the counter. The way I see it, tropical weather is associated with devalued currencies whose buying power is so much less than its weight. Ironically, the more buying power a currency has, the less you need to carry, and the 'best' money of all is actually that great facilitator, the credit card. When shopping in Kaduna my wife and I take along a basketful of naira: no one ever accepts a cheque or a plastic card.

I am reminded of Uganda in the late eighties when, having moved there, I wanted to buy a car. The preliminary transaction was easy. But the deal developed a bottleneck *after* we signed the papers. Not locally employed, I gave a sterling cheque to a friend,

179

who arranged for me to collect millions of Ugandan shillings from his bank. After I had been shown sackfuls of money, I brought along the man from whom I had bought the car, so that he could collect it. Because there had been a spate of daylight stick-ups outside the bank, I wished to have nothing to do with so much cash now that it was no longer mine; but neither did the seller of the car, who refused to hand over the car keys until the money was safely his. (At the time no one would accept cheques, and Museveni's government had passed draconian laws punishing anyone who knowingly bounced a cheque in payment for goods or services already received or rendered. Cash was therefore the only honoured form of exchange.) The deal might have been called off if an acquaintance of mine hadn't found someone who knew a third party who in turn could facilitate the handing over of the money to the man from whom I had bought the vehicle without it leaving the bank.

I paid the third party, the fixer, a percentage to 'encourage' the deputy-manager of the bank where the money was held to 'communicate' with the deputy-manager of the bank to which it would be transferred. All this took minutes; then I was the proud owner of a car, and its seller the happy recipient of money.

Barclays was the first bank established in West Africa, in 1894, while the National and Grindlays Banks operated in East, South and Central Africa, trading in currencies, lending money and encouraging local farmers to produce cash crops. In the main, these banks imported British Indian rupees, which were converted first to paper florin and then to the shilling coin.

Part of the imperial economic thrust, the banks impeded development in Africa by investing all their money in England and by promoting development in Britain at the expense of the poor colonies. And when lending, the banks discriminated against Africans, preferring whites and Asians.

As functioning institutions, banks must, of necessity, operate in an atmosphere of mutual trust: the party depositing or borrowing money signs on the dotted line with utter faith. The trouble is that no one appears to trust anyone any more, especially in Africa. Gone are the days when societies were trustful of one another's spoken word, or had faith in one another's signed affidavits. And the value of money has declined in line with one's trust in money matters. Distrusting banks and one another, many Africans keep their money at home, under the mattress or locked away in safes; some bury their savings in the ground, running the risk of losing their wealth altogether.

This mistrust is reflected in every transaction, however simple. When I lived in Uganda, my Kampalan friends warned me to avoid handling Ugandan paper money, believing that one could get Aids from it. On no account, one of them said, should I lick my index finger and thumb when counting it. I didn't believe this, but, finding the whole business a most tedious affair, I did my cautious best not to touch it myself, giving wads of it tied with rubber-bands to whomever I was buying things from, whom I would ask to count it. I've begun to do the same here in Kaduna.

In Zimbabwe, during my last, brief visit, I experienced distrust of a different kind. I went to ZimBank to change one hundred and fifty American dollars. I handed the money over the counter to a woman cashier, who, taking it from me, made me fill in a form and then vanished, returning several minutes later to inform me that my fifty-dollar bill was counterfeit. Refusing to be taken in by that, I made a scene, pointing out that the bills had been issued to me by my London bank. Rudely, the woman insinuated that although I might not be a dealer in counterfeit money, the bill could be used as evidence against me. I reiterated that *my* fifty-dollar bill was 'good', and perhaps someone had replaced it with a bad one. Becoming ruder, she reminded me that it was my word against hers and threatened to call the police, who would see to it that I was punished. I had no wish to spend even a minute at a Zimbabwean police station, so I accepted the most crudely forged bill I've ever seen, and gave her another, this time requesting that she stay within my view.

I remain impressed by the impertinence of the ZimBank cashier who had no qualms about insisting that my London bank had issued such an outrageous forgery. Or could it be that a British bank clerk had knowingly slipped it in, confident that no one would ever suspect?

That's what money does to one: makes one suspicious.

William Wharton
WRONGFUL
DEATHS

TRUTH: On 3 August 1988 William Wharton's first born child –
along with her husband and two daughters – died in a stubble fire
that engulfed Interstate Highway 5 in Oregon and resulted in an
accident involving forty vehicles.

TRUTH: She and her husband, three days after they had 'died',
visited William Wharton, who was asked to do things that stretch
the limits of compassion and despair.

TRUTH: Someone is to blame for their deaths. But who?

Wrongful Deaths is the powerful story of losing a family; of justice,
of right and wrong, and of truth.

Hardcover £14.99

GRANTA BOOKS

GRANTA

DAVID KYNASTON
PLAYING THE GAME:
THE CITY

No kind of conversation known to man can for a
moment compete in point of dullness with the habitual
discourse of the genuine City Man. What is so and so
worth? What did he start with? How much did he lose in
Kaffirs? What did he give for that place he bought in
Kent? How has he been doing at Newmarket? How long
will he be able to keep it up at this rate? Did he get any
money with his wife? What does he give his daughters?
And so the stream flows on. It takes its rise in money;
through money it runs its course; in money it ends; but
only ends to begin again tomorrow.

George Russell, *Social Silhouettes*, 1906

In the 1980s, life in the City of London changed. The market
floor gave way to the electronic screen; the leisurely lunch was
replaced by the designer sandwich; small, privately-owned firms
gave way to huge, globally-ambitious banking corporations.
Fortunes were made, and the acronym BOBO was coined ('Burnt
Out But Opulent'). The Big Bang of 1986, imposed by the
Thatcher government on a reluctant City, was a conscious—and
successful—attempt to ensure London's future as an international
financial centre, deregulating the Stock Exchange and opening its
firms up to outside ownership. It was also, like so much of
Thatcherism, an attempt to return to the nineteenth century, the
pre-1914 world of minimal government interference, unfettered
market forces and Dickensian extremes of wealth and poverty,
happiness and sorrow.

The late nineteenth century was when the City of London
was at the height of its powers. Amsterdam, formerly the world's
leading financial centre, had lost its position as a result of the
French Revolutionary Wars in 1795, and New York only began
its rise with Britain's economically disastrous decision to fight the
First World War. Furthermore, all the main currencies were
pegged to the international gold standard which, in effect, was
run by the Bank of England from its fortress in Threadneedle
Street. Most of the world's trade relied on making use of the Bill

Opposite: the Stock Exchange during the nineteenth century.

185

of Exchange on London—by which the City's merchant banks, in return for a commission, guaranteed payment for goods—and the Square Mile exported capital to all quarters of the globe, financing governments, railways, mines and all manner of economic activity. The institution that set the City's pulse, that embodied its outlook, that assumed an almost emblematic quality, was the Stock Exchange. The merchant bankers in their august parlours may have sought to dictate the course of high finance, but they were always at the mercy of market sentiment, emanating not just day by day but minute by minute from the floor of the House, as the Stock Exchange was familiarly called. Cycles of boom and slump in the stock market determined the rhythm of *rentier* life. 'Ah, my good woman, it is not the poor only who have their troubles,' ran a *Punch* cartoon of the 1890s showing a dean being importuned for alms by a beggar. 'You, for instance, have probably never experienced the difficulty of finding investments combining adequate security with a remunerative rate of interest.' Not until the 1980s would the Stock Exchange again matter so much.

The late-Victorian Stock Exchange was a club. Its inward-looking character dated back to the 1730s, when the brokers and jobbers of the day were still based in the coffee houses of Change Alley. Legislation attempted to reduce the range of stockbroking business, placing a prohibition on highly profitable 'time bargains' by which traders gambled on future prices without actually buying or selling stock, somewhat analogous to present-day options and derivatives. Confronted by this hostile legislation, the brokers and jobbers simply ignored it and developed their own self-regulating mechanism, in which the sanctity of the bargain was paramount. 'My word is my bond' became no idle boast. From 1773 the Stock Exchange had a permanent home, from 1801 on its present site. Its fortress mentality deepened through the nineteenth century, and a vigorous 'rat-hunt' was liable to ensue if a stranger was spotted inside the House. A public gallery, recommended by a Royal Commission in 1878, was not opened until 1953. A striking paradox was starting to emerge: the Stock Exchange, like the rest of the City, made its living from servicing the ever-changing needs of the world at large, yet it was (and would remain) an extraordinarily conservative institution.

A journalist, W. Arthur Woodward, promised the readers of *Pearson's Magazine* in February 1896 an unprecedented guided tour; he was sneaked in by a member-friend 'on the stipulation that the moment my intrusion was suspected his connection with me ended.' His entrance was through one of the building's seven 'equally unassuming, equally gloomy' doorways, 'zealously guarded by porters in uniforms of dark blue with brass buttons and scarlet collars and gold-braided hats'; once inside, he found 'a vast, lofty chamber' with a 'gilt dome and vaulted roof of glass supported by huge columns of red-brown granite, while the bare marble walls glimmer like polished mirrors under the rays of the electric arc lights suspended from the dome.' Moving towards the centre of the floor, 'at every yard the crowd became denser and the indescribable babel of voices grew louder.' The individual markets, specializing in particular securities, were 'only to be distinguished by the members who form the various groups making denser corners in an already densely crowded room'; in the execution of bargains, 'no written contracts or notes pass between broker and jobber' but instead 'each makes a hasty pencil entry in his pocket-book.' Like any journalist, Woodward needed to ask questions to make sense of what he was seeing; understandably, his nerve failed him, and his account fades disappointingly away.

But Woodward was right to emphasize the individual markets that made up the market as a whole. Some of them, like the Consol market which dealt in British Government stock, were eminently respectable; others, like the American market or the South African mining market (known as the Kaffir Circus), were much less so and had a strong speculative element. The members who manned these markets were the jobbers—some 2,000 men (no women until the 1970s) who, in effect, acted as shopkeepers specializing in particular types of stocks and shares and to whom brokers, acting on behalf of members of the public, came if they wished to buy or sell. The jobbers, far more than the brokers, comprised the heart of the Stock Exchange: they set the tone,

David Kynaston

reacted bullishly or bearishly to the ceaseless swirl of news and
rumours, dispensed the tips, told the jokes and generally ran the
show.

W ho were the jobbers?
There was Tom Nickalls, who dominated the American
('Yankee') market for three decades from the 1860s by sheer force
of personality. He was a burly man with a voice to match. A
contemporary affirmed:

> He has any amount of pluck, taking a view and acting
> on it, sublimely disregarding the minute calculations on
> which smaller speculators pin their faith. It is no use
> talking to him about figures or dividends. 'Who is
> buying?' or 'Who is selling?' he asks, and then makes up
> his mind what to do.

In the late 1890s he was succeeded by Tootie Brander, a
prominent figure not only in the House but also just outside in
Shorter's Court, where the Yankee market adjourned for after-
hours dealing while the wires were still coming over from New
York. Convivial, sleek and good at bluffing, he also had a delicate
touch—in February 1898 a financial gossip column noted that 'It
was very pretty to see the way he picked up a small line of Union
Pacifics the other evening at 34 5/8 after they had refused to sell
them to him nearly a 1/2 dollar higher.' Tootie died at his home in
Hampstead in 1901 at the age of forty-three, leaving almost
£22,000 (about a million in today's money).

And there was Harry Paxton, elephantine in build, a jobber
who more or less lasted the course. A Stock Exchange member
since 1878, he migrated in 1894 from Yankees to Kaffirs, and the
following spring, with the boom in South African gold-mining
shares at its most feverish, he fought what became known as the
'Battle of Throgmorton Street'.

Late every afternoon there were after-hours dealings in
Throgmorton Street, a narrow thoroughfare next to the Stock
Exchange. The police started charging members with obstruction
and hiring empty cabs to go up and down the street. Paxton
('Packy') then went on the offensive. One day he took possession

188

Photo: Guildhall Library, Corporation of London

Above: Throgmorton Street in 1905.

189

David Kynaston

of a cab and drove up and down the street to cheering crowds; another day he shouted loudly and provocatively, 'Who pays for those cabs?' and eventually, amid much scuffling and disorder, he was arrested. The next morning, at the Guildhall Police Court, Mr Alderman Bell declared that Paxton and his fellow-members had turned Throgmorton Street into 'a bear garden', but declined to punish the defendant, and the corpulent jobber 'left the court in the company of his friends, who, on getting outside, cheered heartily.' The episode established him as a Stock Exchange hero, but the rest of his career was an anti-climax. By the turn of the century, he was scratching a living in the Russian mining market; his wife, daughter and son-in-law all predeceased him; and on 23 December 1916, intending to spend Christmas in Brighton, favourite haunt of Stock Exchange men, he was taken ill in the train, assisted out and, at the age of sixty, died on Victoria Station.

Jobbers could be thrown into confusion by the most insignificant of unforeseen events. In August 1896, for instance, the American market was wholly nonplussed by a presidential candidate's speech on silver: for five minutes the members did nothing, waiting for each other to make a move, not even venturing to make a price on straightforward stocks. Lawrence Jones, a merchant banker who came to the City just before the First World War, observed in his memoirs:

The idea that stock-jobbers have secret sources of information and . . . mark the prices of their wares up and down accordingly is of course moonshine. They take the same interest in public affairs as the rest of us, no more nor less, and have the same sources of information, which is usually the press.

The point holds for the present-day City, and the continuing cultivation of mystique helps to rationalize—and smokescreen—indecently high levels of remuneration.

A jobber needed to establish good relations with brokers to establish a profitable network of clients, but there was nothing quite so helpful as the family tie, given that most jobbing and broking firms were tightly-controlled family businesses. Beyond family lay the whole critical area of personal influence and

190

connection. A member with no connections could get by provided he established a reputation for *something*: sport was best (many well-known amateur cricketers secured berths with firms eager to exploit their flannelled prowess), but one Percy Marsden (nicknamed, as his initials would suggest, 'Good Afternoon') made capital out of his resemblance to Edward VII; at weekends he would ride along the Brighton sea-front in a landau and wave a laconic hand to the cheering crowds. Harry Panmure Gordon, a leading broker, was the supreme self-publicist; his homes in London, Brighton and Hertfordshire were lavish affairs in which he entertained freely; he was reckoned to have the best private collection of carriages in the world; and he possessed more than a thousand neckties. 'I shall live a rich man and die a poor one,' he once remarked, computing that his minimum expenditure was £2,000 a month (about £100,000 today). His way of life, coupled with an engaging personality, enabled him to mix with the cream of society and gave him an entry into the best City parlours. The financial brain of his firm was actually a rather dour Belgian called Willie Koch, but 'PG' was the man everyone talked about.

As a club, the Stock Exchange in its late-Victorian heyday indulged in a predictably hermetic language. Nicknames were rife, usually with a readily apparent schoolboy logic behind the tag. 'Cream-jugs' were Charkow-Krementschug Railway bonds, 'Ducks' were Aylesbury Dairy Co. shares, 'Haddocks' were Great North of Scotland ordinary stock, 'Sardines' were Royal Sardinian Railway shares, 'Sarah's Boots' were Sierra Buttes Gold Mine shares and so on. As for members' own sobriquets, most fell in the 'Packy' class of inventiveness, but there were a couple of examples of genuine wit. One member was nicknamed 'Channel Tunnel' because he was reckoned the greatest bore on earth. Another, Louis Fleischmann, was known as 'Louis XIV' because the only time he was invited to dinner was when someone else had dropped out, and he was roped in by a desperate hostess. Fleischmann was a Jew, but there was rarely more than an undertow of anti-Semitism in the Stock Exchange; this was amply compensated for by a host of other prejudices. When the first black clerk made his appearance in the House, he was serenaded with 'Down where the Darkies are a'Weepin''. When a young member appeared one morning dressed in a light brown suit rather than the regulation black, he was seized and frog-marched out. When a leading jobber failed to stand champagne all round the market on the day of his son's wedding, the offended jobbers formed a syndicate and presented his junior partner with half-a-dozen bottles of ginger beer. At the start of the Boer War, when a member failed to keep a place open for a clerk who had gone to the front, he was thrown to the floor and kicked in the face. And in the hushed atmosphere on the morning after the death of Queen Victoria, a broker went into the Yankee market to ask the price of Milwaukees and got his hat smashed for daring to think of business. Only the foolish and the brave risked offending the code of this particular club.

The muscular ethos was that of the public school, and the Stock Exchange was a place where overgrown schoolboys could indulge in a series of japes with little fear of punishment. In December 1890, after a fire made of *Daily Graphic*s had broken out in the American market, a witness told the ruling committee:

> The burning of the papers was a practical joke intended to dislodge him and another member from the seats in question, and that it had the desired effect. He considered that it was a very serious matter, and that he would gladly do all he could to prevent its repetition, but did not see his way to any effectual measures. The number of members engaged in such acts was too great to allow of any personal interference.

It was when business was slack that elderly or unpopular members had to be on their guard against paper balls, paper darts and worse. During the dog days of high summer in 1892, with most of the market leaders away, such was the listlessness that one group of dealers spent whole afternoons standing around waiting for people to trip over a piece of string. Psychologically as well as physically, the life was an unhealthy one and, not surprisingly, as the markets oscillated over the years between feast and famine, the Stock Exchange did not always send out the most rational investment signals.

The tribal behaviour, the institutionalized horseplay, the conspicuous consumption were, at some level, the necessary antidotes to what otherwise would have been corrosive fear. Given the febrile nature of the business, one could hardly expect otherwise. Most members could not get out and in any case were not qualified to do anything else. One who did manage to escape was Francis Carruthers Gould, a member for more than twenty years, who established his reputation through a gift for caricature, finding ample fodder close at hand. During the second half of his life he became a prominent political cartoonist. He looked back on his Stock Exchange years with some affection, claiming that 'a more generous and kindly community of men it would be impossible to find.' But he had no regrets:

> It was like living on a tropical volcanic island; when the sun shone and things went smoothly it was pleasant enough but there were too many sudden and unforeseen bolts from the blue. One might leave the City one evening with everything calm and serene, and the next morning there might be a wild storm with earthquakes and eruptions and panics when the very foundations were shaken, and the crowd in the House, which had been merry and playful in the absence of care only a few hours before, were haggard with anxiety. Some men made fortunes swiftly, some plodded on cautiously, content merely to make a living, whilst others fell by the way. Some were fortunate or skilful enough to weather all the storms and even to profit by them, but there were others whose tragic fate it was to work all their lives only to fail at the end.

Suicides were unnervingly frequent. Montague Spier, a broker, shot himself in the head at the Covent Garden Hotel in February 1893. 'With the few hours of life that still remain I believe I can see clearly and duly estimate the correctness of my judgement, and I still believe I was right as to the value of Italian stock,' he wrote to his clerk in justification of his unfortunate speculations. In November 1895, following a sharp slump in Kaffirs, Frederick Heath was found in a train with his throat slit;

David Kynaston

at the inquest it emerged that he 'had been unable to sleep for the
past three weeks owing to trouble caused by heavy monetary
losses.' Seven years later, following another unexpected relapse in
South African gold-mining shares, the Kaffir jobber Henry Heppel
went down to the lavatory in the Stock Exchange's basement,
locked himself in a stall and blew his brains out with an army
revolver. The bullet passed through a partition and wounded
another member in the arm. 'I have speculated madly on this
Account, and am ruined,' read the note that was found on his
body. Less than a fortnight later, a member called George Bennett
killed himself at his home in Richmond, having told his wife the
previous evening that he had 'sustained some financial loss'. A
neighbour revealed at the inquest that Bennett had told him 'that
he did not believe in the future state, and that he worshipped
money.' How many members *did* believe in the future state?

The collective unconscious was ruled over by the sound of a
hammer being brought down three times on a wooden surface.
The ceremony was simple and all too familiar. If a member failed,
an attendant would climb the rostrum, rap sharply three times with
a hammer and, in front of a tense, silent crowd, make the formal
announcement: 'Gentlemen, Mr X begs to inform the House that
he is unable to comply with his bargains.' A letter posted on 1
September 1911, written by John Braithwaite, son of the senior
partner of a highly reputable firm, testifies to the feelings of
panic under the Exchange's robust surface:

> Look at the price we have paid for meddling in Oil! We
> have suffered great financial loss and still worse we have
> ruined our reputation with those who followed us into
> Oil. We know nothing about it yet we presumed to pose
> as competent advisers. What induced us to do it? Many
> causes no doubt; but partly I fear the vanity of the
> thought that we were Great Company Brokers—would-
> be Pioneer Oil Brokers!
>
> You may perhaps be surprised that I have spoken of
> the possibility of failure. It is because it has been before
> my mind like a nightmare day and night more or less

continuously for the last month and more—I have suffered it all mentally over and over again—when the hammer has gone in the House it has sounded like a knell in my ears—I have thought of the long list of our names and the awful staggering hush afterwards.

In the event, the firm survived, Braithwaite eventually becoming Chairman of the Stock Exchange and receiving a knighthood.

This unstable existence sometimes took its toll on relations between members; there were plenty of rows on the floor of the House, ranging from slanging matches to punch-ups. 'You have made statements about my dealings which are false and you are a damned liar and a bloody cad and now take me before the Committee': so in February 1902 Douglas Uzielli, a particularly noisy and aggressive jobber in the Kaffir Circus, upbraided his fellow-jobber Harry Mosenthal, who had been heard rubbishing the credit of Uzielli's firm. Yet on the whole there seems to have been a solidarity and camaraderie between members—provided, of course, a member was not a radical or a puritan or wore his hair too long. It was as if, at the mercy of forces beyond their control, members derived some comfort from maintaining a united front. A jobber called Murray Griffith entitled his memoirs *Forty Years in the Best Club in London*; for him, the Stock Exchange had been an exciting, even exhilarating way of life fortified by the good fellowship of the club to which he was proud to belong:

I have always considered that the Stock Exchange is the real and true example of a socialistic institution, inasmuch that it gives everyone a chance of getting on, if he has the energy and brains so to do. Again, I say they ask no questions; you do not require a banker's reference, etc., all you have to do is to 'play the game'; and even if a man is unfortunate and comes to an end financially, it is not a question of how he came to grief, 'but did he play the game?'

GRANTA

WILL HUTTON
PLAYING THE GAME:
THE TAKEOVER

Hanson plc is a British success story. Set up in 1965, it has grown by takeover; in 1990, Lord Hanson, founder and chairman, could claim twenty-five years of uninterrupted profits and dividend growth. Today, Hanson plc has a ten-billion-pound turnover and employs eighty thousand people.

How is such success possible?

The product is the secondary factor in the immensely profitable equation. Indeed, it is the proud boast of Lord White, Lord Hanson's partner, that he has never even set foot on the shop floor of any of the companies that he has bought—and there are a great many, because acquiring companies is how Hanson plc makes money. It is an operation driven entirely by manipulating the possibilities afforded by Britain's financial structures.

Hanson's 1982 takeover of the British company Berec, manufacturer of Ever Ready batteries, illustrates how such manipulation pays off. Immediately following the £95 million takeover, Hanson sold Berec's European divisions to Duracell, Berec's chief competitor, for £37 million, thus recouping two-fifths of its initial outlay. In the British market, the price of Berec's products was pushed up—Hanson wanted to see profits as quickly as possible—with the result that sales stagnated. Hanson also insisted that any future investment it made in Berec would have to meet a staggeringly high target return. By 1992, Ever Ready had lost its position as the market leader in Britain; Hanson then sold Berec to another competitor, Ralston Purina, for £132 million, only fractionally less, allowing for inflation, than Hanson had paid for it. The verdict of the new owners on their acquisition was unequivocal: they described it as 'a business in decline'.

For Hanson, the running down of the company made perfect financial sense. Hanson plc more than recovered its investment. Before the takeover, Berec had been trying to build a global business, investing heavily in research and development. Ten years of the Hanson treatment left it a shell. But that was of no consequence; Hanson plc made its money.

It is difficult to see how it can be argued that these methods

Opposite: Lord Hanson.

are beneficial to British business, yet they have many defenders. Hanson plc is said to be the model of modern British capitalism, shaking up sleepy managements and—since it might strike anywhere—responsible for a general improvement in efficiency that can only be engendered by fear.

The Berec story is one that is repeated week by week and month by month across the swathe of British business. Regarded as the norm, it is actually the product of Britain's extraordinary financial and corporate structures, which have developed over the past three hundred years and are underpinned by an intricate and distinctive value system.

The first defender of Hanson-esque capitalism is the Conservative Party. One of the Party's remarkable features is that it is often regarded almost as a non-political organization. In the Conservative heartlands of England, the Party is like the Townswomen's Guild or the Chamber of Commerce. Its agenda is not seen as radical or extreme; it is merely an expression of the way things are and ought to be. Part of the historic point of Conservatism is to occupy office to prevent others from making changes.

The Conservative Party is also the *gentleman's* party, and the gentlemanly ideal was one of the animating forces in the rise of British capitalism. Historically, the English aristocrat lived on rents from his land; with only a finite amount of land available, the aspiring gentleman had to find another suitable source of income—that is, an income for which one did not labour too obviously. The interest, dividends and profits from finance and commerce soon became the best alternative to rolling acres in the shires.

The gentlemanly ideal also embraces a certain kind of bearing. A gentleman does not try too hard, is understated in his approach to life, celebrates sports, games and pleasure; he is fair-minded, has good manners and is steady under fire. A gentleman does not lie, because his word is his bond; he takes a pride in being practical, distrusts foreigners, is public spirited and keeps his distance from his inferiors. The civilization fostered by these values is highly favourable to finance and commerce, and unfavourable to manufacturing industry. Gentlemanliness is a set of clichés, but it is also a powerful ideology.

The monarchy has always been the focus of the social hierarchy, and even now, in the late twentieth century, the Court still plays an important role in gentlemanly life. The aristocracy continues to serve the Queen in a series of functions with ridiculous names—Silver Sticks, Crown Equerries. The pomp, the ceremony and the 'heritage' appeal combine to mask the political and social importance of such informal Conservative networks. Landowners, the military and old City families congregate at this centre of Conservative England; their connections offer them advancement in regiments, in City investment houses, in the Inns of Court and in boardrooms.

The entrance tickets to this world remain education and family. The public schools still nurture the Conservative gentleman, combing the intense intellectual and social training that permits both academic success and the badge of gentlemanliness— the common language, the accent of which is the hallmark of good breeding and self-confidence. Manufacturers and rich immigrants aspire to join their ranks.

Competence has always been seen as the prerogative of Conservatives. They set social standards, they govern and they judge. And, in the same way, they manage the economy.

The second important defender of the British financial system is the Bank of England, which is tied firmly to the Conservative establishment. Its governing body is known, appropriately enough, as the Court. There are eighteen directors, six of whom are Bank of England officials. Six more are drawn from other City institutions, like the great merchant banks; the membership is completed by six industrialists (the government declined to renominate a trade unionist in 1994 when the position became vacant). Of the non-Bank members of the Court, five run companies which are major contributors to the Conservative Party. The new Governor is Eddie George, a career Bank of England official.

The Bank of England is the ultimate arbiter of the Stock Market, where company shares can be bought and sold, and the money markets, where banks and other financial institutions can lend each other spare cash. More than three thousand companies are quoted on the Stock Market. The daily turnover is extraordinary: £2.5 billion in British shares, six billion pounds in government bonds, three-quarters of a million contracts bought and sold on the future exchanges. Annual turnover of domestic and foreign equities together exceeds that of any financial centre except New York. For a medium-sized economy such as Britain's, these are staggering numbers.

This churning sea of money has attracted more than five hundred foreign banks to London, allowing it to retain its high rank in the world financial order, despite the weakness of the British economy. So many institutions buying and selling, depositing and borrowing, create the illusion that behind the markets lies a great national economy—a kind of self-perpetuating confidence trick.

London has also become the centre of the new 'derivatives' markets. 'Derivatives' have no claim on real assets and income flows; they are financial instruments dreamed up by bankers and brokers, and their function is to allow the holder to bet on the future price of real assets—exchange rates, the level of the stock market, interest rates in six and twelve months' time. Practically any transaction in the future value of almost any asset can be accommodated, for a price.

Several assumptions inform the Bank of England's philosophy. First, it believes that the Stock Market is an effective way of raising money for companies. Second, it believes that takeovers are an effective means of improving efficiency. Third, it regards low inflation and financial stability as the prime sources of growth. And above all, it believes that the financial institutions are serving the economy well, arguing that if companies demand different kinds of financial support, it will naturally appear—it is, after all, a free market.

These beliefs chime perfectly with the instinctive Conservative bias towards the financial interest at the expense of the producer, benefiting the southern *rentier* rather than the northern manufacturer. These values are so deeply ingrained that they are taken as accepted truths: their practitioners quite possibly no longer recognize their partisanship. The Bank of

England is nominally a public body, nationalized by a Labour government in 1946, but it has never felt any need—and has never been called upon—to qualify its view that what is good for the City must also be in the public interest. The formal role of the Bank of England is not, in fact, to run the City's markets; it is to act as the government's banker, raising money day by day so that the government can pay its bills, and managing the state's foreign exchange reserves and its currency policy. But the Bank's internal organization, its culture and its recruitment policy have made it a powerful presence inside the government, the voice of *laissez-faire* economics, low inflation and sound money.

The core of any financial system is money, and legal tender can only be supplied by the government of the day via its central banks—in Britain the Bank of England.

Cash is permanently available, at a price. If the Bank wishes to change the level of interest rates, it changes that price; if it wants to keep the system short of cash then it charges a premium, signalling to all that if they need liquidity they must pay a penalty. Banks and markets are in a permanent cat-and-mouse game, second-guessing each other over hourly moves in interest rates.

In other countries, central banks actively manage the structure of short-term interest rates from money that is lent for periods of time which vary from twenty-four hours to twenty-five years. But the Bank of England is not interested in intervening so extensively. The British system is a free-for-all, in which as far as possible everything is determined by supply and demand, and cash is always available. The only constraint is its price.

The effect of this policy on Britain's commercial banks—its so-called clearing banks—and consequently on British business is dramatic. The banks know that there will always be cash to borrow, and do not need to worry if they have to pay a premium; they can pass the cost on to their customers. They are forced into keeping their lending as short-term as they can, due to the fluctuating price of money. They also have to ensure that interest rates on the loans they make move in line with the cost of deposits. Prudent banking practice demands that the kind of bank loan financed by short-term borrowing should itself be short-term, with a variable interest rate, secured by collateral (for example your house) which can be confiscated if the borrower defaults. Given these circumstances, it is not very attractive for the clearing banks to lend long-term to industry at a fixed rate of interest.

Comparison with other countries is difficult because British banks do not like to disclose the extent of their short-term lending. One of the few available international comparisons reveals that, in 1992, fifty-eight per cent of all lending to small and medium-sized British companies was in the form of overdrafts—a deficit on a company's bank account, on which the bank can foreclose at any time. This compares with fourteen per cent in Germany, thirty-one per cent in France and thirty-five per cent in Italy. And, of course, virtually the entire stock of British company debt was at variable rates.

British companies are therefore more reluctant to take on loans than their competitors abroad. They do not want to incur debt on the dangerous terms offered by the banks. They must hope to finance investment and research and development through profits. To make sure their internal sources of finance are sufficiently large, British companies are compelled to set high prices, and so lose market share to overseas competitors whose financial structures allow a lower cost of capital. These competitors can climb on to a virtuous circle of expanding output and investment, while British companies are forced into a vicious circle of static output and lagging investment.

Clearing banks are also faced with the problem of their own shareholders setting very demanding targets for the rate of return on their investment. This demand for quick profits is fundamental to the banks' relationship with industry.

In the United States, banks are faced with similar difficulties, but American companies have a wide range of local financial options. Until recently, the US government forbade state banks to lend outside state boundaries, and so companies had a captive banking system, forced to offer attractive terms. The state banks have more knowledge of their customers, their business strategies and their viability; they are not reduced to a series of financial ratios held on the head-office computer, as they are in Britain. They also have a sense of belonging to the cities and regions in which they operate.

If economic decline hits a region, it has adverse effects on the business prospects of a particular bank, but also on the employment prospects of the bankers' associates and relatives. No such emotional pull touches the British system. South Wales or Durham might as well be in Latin America for all the effect their decline has on the directors of Barclays or Lloyds. The London financial institutions make their cold-blooded judgement; it cannot be contested.

The problem is twofold: the terms on which finance is offered to British business by the banks, and the financial returns that the owners of British business require. It leads straight to consideration of the London Stock Market, where titles to ownership of companies—the shares—are bought and sold daily in staggering numbers.

The Stock Market is viewed by the Bank of England, the City institutions and the financial pages of the broadsheet newspapers as a source of great economic strength. The minute-by-minute juggling with financial assets is presented to the nation as a vital function. The Stock Market's health is a pervasive concern, on a par with the weather forecast and the traffic news. Its daily movements, flickering on screens in the London investment houses, are charted by television, radio and the press, and the carousel of bids, deals, takeovers and power plays is the staple of most business-news coverage. Its values are pervasive; the *Financial Times* ranks companies not according to their turnover or assets but by the price of their shares on the Stock Market. Ninety-three of the world's top one thousand companies ranked by Stock Market value are British; if ranked by turnover or assets, this number is more than halved.

Stock Market apologists claim that this restless daily adjustment in prices is beneficial; the market is trying as efficiently as it can to reflect the economic value of all the information it has to hand. It means that company directors have to demonstrate that the maximum is being done to boost profits and dividends, which, it is argued, acts as a spur to efficiency because the directors are always at risk of being expelled by the shareholders.

Above all, there is the threat that the shareholders will sell to a buyer who thinks that more value can be extracted from the assets—the takeover. Takeovers, running at an average of forty a year, are an abiding feature of the London Stock Market. At the height of the boom in 1986 and 1987, some concern was expressed that takeovers were frightening companies into making absurdly high dividend payments and forcing them into focusing only on immediate profitability. But the view that only the market can produce the best outcome for society and individuals alike runs very deep—and it proved impossible to harden the concerns into a programme of reform.

These concerns were well-founded. Faith in takeovers as a means of keeping companies efficient rests on two assumptions. The first is that markets accurately value future returns; the second is that there are no efficiency losses from the continuing re-evaluation of a company's worth. The first assumption is questionable: no one can be counted on to be rational about the future. One of the most robust laws of experimental psychology is that individuals are wildly inconsistent in the way they rank rewards over time, and place a heavy emphasis on rewards in the present. Rewards in the future have to be very much higher than is rational in order to persuade individuals to accept them. This is as true of men in suits as of rats and pigeons. And the second assumption ignores the destructive effects of the endless change of valuation on the long-term relations of a firm with its workers, suppliers and customers.

The issue is not, as Stock Market apologists hysterically insist, that critics of the financial markets are trying to control dividend payments which are the shareholders' legitimate rewards for risk. (In June 1994, Lord Hanson wrote a letter to the Prime Minister saying that any government examination of the level of dividend payments would be a socialist measure.) The issue is that the reward for this risk is disproportionately high; even in the United States, dividends to shareholders as a proportion of a company's profit run at half the British level.

The case against the Stock Market is that its sole yardstick is shareholder value and short-term corporate profitability. It is incapable of placing value on anything else. It takes no account of the wider benefits that the existence of an independent, self-governing firm brings to those who participate in it, or of the co-operative contracts between a firm's various stakeholders that also contribute to its efficiency. Hanson is just an extreme example of a general trend. The company's demand for very high rates of return on its investment, and its insistence that projects finance themselves within four or five years are also the demands of the Stock Market. In the 1970s and early 1980s, Hanson seemed original for making these demands explicit, but now—as surveys by the Confederation of British Industry and the Bank of England both show—they are generalized. Everyone makes them.

It is one of the paradoxes of the British system that these demands stem from the fact that shareholders regard themselves more and more as uncommitted owners, with no obligations to the companies they own. The uncommitted owner is always ready to 'exit', to sell his shares, and so companies have to make ever-higher returns in order to fend off the threat of takeover.

The British financial system has developed over three centuries. London is at the system's heart and has been so since the late seventeenth century: the country's chief port and commercial centre, it is also near the Court and Westminster. Just as the successful City merchant or banker could expect his money to buy a place in society quickly in the eighteenth century, so the same forces are at work today. For three hundred years, a unique political, social and economic constellation has held together, and it remains the foundation of contemporary Conservatism. Court, land and finance—extending outwards to the army—remain the apex of the social and political pyramid and the focus of economic endeavour.

Over the past sixteen years of Conservative government, the authoritarian capabilities of the state have been ruthlessly enlisted to serve the interests of finance, which neatly chimes with long-standing British values and the structure of Britain's institutions. In the name of deregulation, the financial system has become even more market-based and even more centralized in London. Sterling may rank below the dollar, yen, Deutschmark and French and Swiss franc as an international currency, but London's status as the least regulated world financial market has allowed it to become the centre of global finance. The preoccupation with liquidity has been worsened by the slew of 'derivatives', which is now so large that their minute-by-minute price movements make all the real markets much more febrile, in sympathy.

The relationships between individual banks and companies are being eroded, as market-based contracts weaken the flow of information between them upon which the build-up of long-term debt depends. Banks are not interested in strengthening their ties with companies; they are interested in developing new markets in loans so that debt can be bought and sold just like shares. Medium-sized and small companies do not even have the advantage available to large companies of getting their finance, at least initially, on keen terms. Reliant on a banking system that is averse to risk, disengaged and short-term, a small company quoted on the Stock Market has to meet the same dividend requirements as a large one. Even unquoted companies find that they have to meet these requirements if they are preparing for flotation and the personal enrichment of their private owners.

Britain's economic structures are the product of this environment, and from them radiate the effects on everything from employment to housing that bring so much economic inefficiency and social distress. British firms are obliged to economize on labour and 'casualize' as much of their workforce as possible in order to meet the returns that are demanded.

The welfare of a significant part of the population has been damaged by the new regime. The results have fed back into higher government welfare spending and violent economic cycles, a slowing of long-term growth, permanent unemployment, mounting social disorder and the exclusion of growing numbers of people from proper citizenship. There may have been some efficiency gains in a few firms, and more wealth for a few individuals, but these results cannot justify the wider losses. London's financial markets may seem far removed from the disintegration of family life and the decline in the public realm that disfigure contemporary Britain, but they are as linked to them as the remote shocks of an earthquake are to the epicentre.

LARRY FINK
PLAYING THE GAME:
THE PLAYERS

GRANTA

SAM TOPEROFF
MEMORIES OF A UNION MAN

Sam Toperoff

My father used to express his hopes for me while passing through the doorway between his small store in front and our apartment in the rear. He'd talk to my mother as though I wasn't standing right there. 'He's artistic,' he'd say. 'He could become a sign-painter. People always need signs. Pays good money. Tough union to crack, though.'

Then, a week or so later: 'Meat-cutter. People're always going to eat meat, for heaven's sake. Steady work, and he'll make good money if he can get into the union.'

Later still: 'I was talking to Hansen, the plumber. Tells me there's lots of work around. He'd be willing to start him as a helper. If it works out, he'll help him get a union card. Plumbing, it's steady.'

These, and half a dozen other careers, were his great expectations for me. It was the early fifties; I was twelve or thirteen.

My father was a small, disappointed man who ran a foundering candy store in Brooklyn. He worked twelve to fourteen hours each day, seven days a week, barely keeping his family above the low tide of subsistence. Naturally, he wanted a better life for me: to him, that meant job security, 'good' money and a forty-hour week. In other words, a union job. In our neighbourhood, an entire generation of hard-working fathers wanted the same thing for their sons.

Sometimes I wish I had taken my father's union dreams more seriously, but I wasn't a very serious kid. College had never been a real possibility in our family, and so I was more of a ballplayer than a scholar. I thought that when the time came to put aside baseball bat and pick up my lunch pail, I'd be ready. It's what I saw all the older kids do after they finished high school. Either that or join the army. It was my destiny to become a working man sooner or later. And a union job, as my father constantly reminded me, would be better than non-union.

I had been stamped 'union made' by my father one day in May 1946. I was only seven. My father told me he intended to close the store the following day—even though he only locked its doors on the highest of Jewish holy days. I'd also be kept out of school, an equally amazing turn of events. He told me that we were going

218

to do something I probably wouldn't understand until I was grown-up. I was prepared for something dull and educational.

As we walked to the station, I thought that the day wouldn't be a total waste: the train crossed over the East River on the Manhattan Bridge. At least I would get to see the water and the skyscrapers.

We got off at the Union Square. It was where my mom took me to buy school pants each fall, to S. Klein's 'On the Square', a chaotic, low-priced department store I detested. My father and I walked up to street level and into a crowd consisting of men a lot like my father, in suits and hats, but without ties. Wooden horses blocked off lower Fifth Avenue, diverting cars and buses. Men milled about between Fourteenth and Sixteenth Street. Many held placards. A ruddy-faced policeman mounted on a dappled chestnut winked at me as we approached the park. He was a cop, so I didn't wink back. We passed vendors—ice-cream and Italian ices, sodas, hot dogs, pretzels, popcorn. I wanted an American flag to wave; instead, my father bought me a button that read SOLIDARITY FOREVER.

A man nearby was inflating and stringing balloons. I didn't want to ask for anything else, but I *really* wanted a balloon. It turned out they weren't for sale; the man was giving them away. My father pushed me forward, and the man tied a yellow balloon to my wrist. Maybe I'd been mistaken and my father had actually brought me someplace fun. I asked him what was happening.

'May Day,' he said. 'Working people all over the world celebrate May Day.'

I thought I already knew all the good holidays.

A group of kids surrounded a man dressed like a shabby clown, who was folding and rolling up a copy of *PM*, a leftist newspaper, my father's favourite. The clown began pulling at the paper tube, bending and tearing it around the edges. He asked, 'Anyone know what newspaper this is?'

'*PM*,' I blurted.

'What if I were to tell you, young fellow'—a few more rips and tugs—'it isn't a newspaper at all? What if I were to show you'—tearing furiously at the paper until, with a blur of jerky movements, he gave a triumphant flourish—'a bouquet of

219

flowers!' The newspaper had become a graceful bunch of stems and newsprint blossoms. I'd never seen anything so magical in my life. 'Here, son.' And I had a bouquet to go with the balloon.

The crowd thickened near the centre of the park. We pushed our way to the speakers' platform. Three people—one a tall black woman in crimson robes—stood around a man with a guitar. They sang 'Look for the Union Label'. My father surprised me again. I was tall for seven; he was short for forty; nevertheless, he whisked me up on to his shoulders. I could see everything—the performers; some low, grey clouds forming over New Jersey; curious faces peering down from the windows overlooking the park; the mass of bobbing hats all around us; lines of policemen at the edges of the crowd. My balloon tugged at my wrist.

I was one of the first to see them coming—a group of men converging on the park. Burly men, none wearing suits or carrying placards. I saw their clubs and lengths of pipe and pulled on a tuft of my father's hair. He brushed my hand away.

The hum from the rear of the crowd sounded like an animal lowing, sensing danger. Then it stopped, or almost stopped, and that was when I became frightened. The thugs entered the crowd, with fists and clubs swinging. I saw hands and arms raised to ward off the blows. I heard screams and thuds. Bodies toppled; people ran; and the crowd recoiled against itself, pushing us forward.

One of the singers was pointing behind us and shouting, 'Stop them! Make them stop!' We tried to run. My father could not see what was happening. I tried to tell him, but I had no words. The singer shouted, 'Police! Police! Police!'

We were pinned against the platform. I felt my father's strong hands squeeze my thighs. I saw some of the clubbings clearly, men with bloodied heads driven to their knees.

The fighting was getting closer and closer. Release finally came from the side, where a section of the crowd broke away and ran eastward down Fifteenth Street. My father ran too, and I bounced on his shoulders in a wild pony ride. I clutched his neck, an ear, his chin, a cheek. I turned round for one last, irresistible look at the mayhem.

My first job was at L & L Woodworking, a small company in Queens that made mouldings. I worked nights, after school. It was 1954. There was no union in the shop.

After a couple of weeks loading and unloading delivery trucks and another few weeks bringing the band-saw operators their wood and watching them feed it into the machines, I got a chance to work on the simplest moulding myself, a ceiling trim with a few clean scallops. The wood was pine, and I had to hold my line for seven-and-a-half feet, watching my fingers carefully for the last few inches.

As time went by, I worked my way up to more complex cuts until I could run a sea-shell design on red oak without any problem. I derived great satisfaction from turning out perfectly-finished pieces. But everything else about the job stank. The sawdust clogged my nose. The shop was freezing in winter, steaming in summer, and my goggles fogged regardless of the season. The whirr of the band-saws was deafening. I made a dollar thirty-five an hour.

Almost forty years after the fact, I realized that Andy Garafola, the guy who broke me in—I considered him old; he was around fifty—had been let go because I eventually worked faster than he did and because I was cheaper. Whoever made such decisions must have figured I'd be at L & L for a long time. My father had other ideas.

Through one of his customers, I got a job as an apprentice at a printing plant, Pandick Press, near Wall Street. It paid about the same money as L & L Woodworking, but held out the promise of membership of the printers' union. My father's eyes shone darkly: 'The Big Six is one of the most powerful unions in the country. If you're there long enough to become a journeyman, it means you can get work anywhere in America where they need printers.' He said it a lot. But I wasn't thinking of journeying. I took the job mostly to make my father happy.

The hours were tough. Lobster shift—six p.m. till two a.m. The bus and subway took more than an hour each way. I was still in high school, and my mother got called in by my teachers on two occasions because I fell asleep in art class and music appreciation. My senior year is a foggy memory.

The work was interesting, especially the rush jobs. I stood in the steamy linotype room, waiting for the hot slugs to tumble out of the machine and be set in a one-page block, which I raced to the proof press on my metal dolly. Then I ran the sample page to the proofreader—he used a bottle of Four Roses bourbon as a paperweight—and flew back to the printer with the pages corrected. I took pride in my speed and my title—a printer's devil.

My mother didn't like that I was always tired or that I was working with so many hard-drinking men. She was overruled by my father, who saw his hopes for his son fulfilled when, after six months, I received my union membership card.

I was drafted a year later. When I got out of the army, I had to choose between my old union job at Pandick Press and going to college, which would be paid for by the GI Bill. My father would have steered me to the printing trade, but he died while I was away. In the army, I had become an avid reader, seduced by books. I chose college.

I became an English professor, and by the late 1970s was teaching at a small liberal arts college. One year my colleagues and I became unhappy with our salary and conditions, and I found myself on a committee organized to address the problems. The committee's first task was to draft a statement defining a professor's function—words like 'educator', 'facilitator' and 'pedagogue' were debated for hours. When I suggested that since we performed tasks for a salary, we really ought to consider ourselves 'workers'. It was as though I'd farted.

The group that was finally formed to represent the professors called itself an 'Association'. Because it refused to call itself a union, it could never really *be* a union. Such snobbery also drove away the non-teaching college staff—secretaries and plant workers mostly—who joined a Teamsters' local.

My heart was never really in my 'Association', even though I was required to pay dues and have it represent me. And then one year, 1976, the Association agreed to work without a contract. I argued at one meeting that a strike, or at least the threat of one, was the only leverage an organized workforce had. (My father would have been proud of me.) I was outvoted and told that I didn't understand the subtleties of negotiations in academia.

I painted the sandwich-board that night. It read: WHAT IS MY SALARY? WILL IT SUPPORT MY FAMILY? WHY NOT JOIN ME?

I met my classes and kept my office hours, but every lunchtime I donned my sandwich-board and walked up and down on the path in front of the president's office.

Walking my one-man picket line, I felt dumb. I felt dumber still because both students and colleagues averted their eyes when they walked by me. I also noticed that people who knew me well altered their route when they saw me, crossing the street or ducking behind the building. Embarrassment—theirs and my own—was a feature of the experience. It was not a graceful matter, making public your desire to have more money.

That first day a couple of students asked me haltingly what I was trying to accomplish. I wanted my union and my bosses to produce a contract under the terms of which I was willing to work, I explained.

One lunchtime, after a week of picketing, a police car pulled up to the kerb. I anticipated a confrontation that would break cleanly along traditional labour struggle lines—crude cop bullies, noble picket. The policeman who got out was a young black man. He apologized profusely for what he was about to do and then escorted me across the street, off university property. No longer on my own turf, I felt instantly absurd. I resolved to call the local newspaper about harassment, but just then school's vice-president, a man I played touch football with, arrived and invited me back on campus to continue my protest.

I picketed the next week, feeling more like a crank than a principled working man with each passing day. Toward the end of the week, a colleague, one of the school's most respected teachers, approached me, shook my hand and said, 'I admire what you're doing, and if there's no contract by next week, I'll be right out here with you.' I took heart.

There was no contract the next week, nor the week after that. But my colleague never joined me on the line. Nobody did. One snowy morning, my wife finally convinced me that I had made my point.

Perhaps I had realized that a protesting intellectual—no matter how profoundly committed he is to the working man's struggle—just isn't the same as a picketing printer or plumber or meat-cutter.

During 1980, a sabbatical year, my wife and daughter and I lived in a French Alpine village. The village was so small that my daughter, Olivia, was one of only ten students enrolled in the local school.

I was surprised one Sunday morning in early May when her *institutresse*, a dour woman in her fifties, knocked on our door. Over coffee, she told me that the Minister of Education had announced a plan to close all rural one-room schoolhouses with fewer than twelve students. The teachers in the region planned a protest march in front of the Ministry office in Gap, a larger town fifteen kilometres away. She wanted to know if I'd come along in a show of parental support. '*Mais oui, madame,*' I cooed.

I wanted to take Olivia, who was seven, with me—repeating with my own child the May Day lesson my father had given me. I expected a token protest: a walk around the Gap town hall, a genteel demonstration of teacher unity and then a reflective bus ride home. I told Olivia that we were going to do something the next day that she probably wouldn't understand until she was grown-up.

On the bus ride to Gap, I was surprised to see that we were the only parent and child present. The teachers, most of them older women, sang children's songs charmingly. Olivia sang along.

The bus did pull up in the Gap town square, but all was not serene. There was a strident, moiling mass of protestors, a few with bullhorns, many waving placards. The national teachers' union had called out every member in the region. They chanted slogans: 'Don't let the fools close down the schools,' which rhymed in French too. Olivia, wide-eyed, grabbed my hand.

The street in front of the town hall was crammed with teachers and their supporters. From the steps, a man began to speak into a microphone. I hoisted Olivia up on my shoulders. I missed the odd French word, but basically it was the same old idiom I'd heard in Union Square. I turned around to see if the goons were coming.

When the speech ended, Olivia and everyone around me picked up the schools–fools chant again. I found myself linking arms with two small women, teachers I didn't even know. We began to march through the town, now singing 'We Shall Overcome' in French. Olivia clutched my hair. I noticed people leaning out of upper-storey windows, wearing expressions ranging from curiosity to disgust. My life in labour had taken a bizarre, international turn.

When we reached the rue Carnot, a busy street and part of a major route that ran from Italy to Aix-en-Provence, the crowd proceeded to stop traffic. The demure women either side of me placed themselves—and, of necessity, me, with my daughter on my shoulders—in front of a huge, refrigerated truck, stopping it dead. The driver, a squat man with a droopy moustache, shouted, 'I'm union too, but I've got to get to Aix.'

The women said, 'No one moves.' Olivia said, 'No one moves.' We all sat down on the cobbles before his bumper. Nothing moved.

Horns began honking, tentatively at first, and then with a noisy persistence, until I could hear them coming from miles away. After a very long while, the *gendarmes* arrived. Initially, they tried to persuade the teachers to move. Then they began to drag some of the protestors away.

Everyone was quiet on the ride back to our village. When I stepped off the bus, I was thanked profusely for my support. Thereafter, Olivia was treated like a little heroine.

There are no more May Days. My daughter is grown and in college; we still laugh occasionally about the teacher protest in Gap. But she's not a union person and probably never will be. Most one-room schoolhouses in France have been closed.

This brave new NAFTA-esque, GATT-arian world doesn't seem like the proper place to write longingly about labour unions. But that's why I've done it. Intellectual or not, I am my father's son and my daughter's father, still a believer in causes; as a misplaced, misbegotten union man, my causes are mostly lost.

I came upon my old WHAT IS MY SALARY? sandwich-board in the attic recently. The romantic in me welled instantly, and I imagined a father—an Asian, a Latino, an Eastern European father, someone who wished for his son or daughter 'good' money, job security, a forty-hour week. I conjured up many such fathers. And millions of their children.

Get a new Perspective on architecture and save 30%

A celebration of the best of the world's architecture and a forum for campaigning against the worst, *Perspectives* is the first magazine on architecture and the environment written specifically with the non-professional in mind.

Informative, lively and controversial, it examines how architecture affects our lives, with in-depth features on the world's finest buildings, taking a critical view of development and planning policy, giving a voice to the architectural community and helping with ideas for the home.

With its stunning full-colour illustrations, *Perspectives* is as beautiful as it is interesting.

GRANTA

JOHN MCGAHERN
CREATURES OF THE EARTH

In wild, wet January weather, two months after Mr Waldron's death, Mrs Waldron and her daughter, Eileen, closed their big house outside Castlebar and moved to their summer cottage on Achill.

The whole family—two other daughters, their husbands, two sons, their wives and three grandchildren—had gathered in the big house that Christmas. They would have preferred it to be kept open until at least the summer, but their mother was determined to move, even on her own. The Waldrons were an unusual family, all of them secure in good professions, and they had little interest in their inheritance other than for it to be settled according to their parents' wishes. Their chief inheritance, a good education, had already been given. Michael Flynn was to be kept on two days a week to look after the gardens and grounds, and Eileen, a solicitor, who worked in Castlebar, might sometimes use the house in bad weather or whenever there were late court sittings. With some reluctance it was agreed that the horses and the few cattle that had been their father's main diversion would be sold. In a year's time they could look at the situation again. With relief and some nervous laughter it was settled that nothing more had to be done or said. They could start opening the wines they would have with the Christmas dinner.

Eileen would have been as happy to stay as to move. There was a man her own age in Castlebar who interested her. It was she who had been the closest to her father. She did not like the idea at first of his horses being sold, but had to admit that keeping them made little sense. Secretly she was glad of the hour-long drive from Achill to Castlebar: it might help shake off the listlessness and sense of emptiness she had begun to feel once her initial anger at the death had passed. And she had come to that unnerving time when youth is rapidly disappearing into early middle age.

The wind rocked the heavy, white Mercedes as they crossed the Sound to the island the January Saturday they moved, the sea and sky rain-sodden and wild. They had taken very little with them from Castlebar. The only precious thing they took was an old, trusting black cat they were all very attached to. The black cat had four white paws and a white star on her forehead and was called Fats.

In the evenings the cat used to wait for the surgeon's car to come from the hospital. Often Mr Waldron carried her indoors on his shoulder, and when he went over the fields to look at the cattle or horses the cat went with him, racing ahead and crying to be lifted on to his shoulder whenever the grass was wet. All through his final illness the cat slept at the foot of his bed. Whenever Mrs Waldron attempted to remove her from the folded quilt, he woke instantly. 'No. Leave her be. *She* has not deserted us'—a humorous reference to the apparent avoidance of them early in the illness, especially by many of the people who had worked for years with him at the hospital. All through their long life together it had been agreed that it was vanity, a waste, to consider how they appeared in the eyes of others.

In merriment they had often recalled walking behind the professor of philosophy on a clear winter's morning when they were undergraduates on their way to the Saturday market and hearing him demand after each person passed, 'Did they *snub* us or did they *not* see us?' Over the years it had become one of the playful catch-phrases of the house: 'Did they not see us or did they *snub* us?'

At first Mrs Waldron did not believe that his colleagues were avoiding him, thought indeed it was all in his imagination: 'You'll be as paranoiac as old Professor Ryan soon if you're not careful.'

'I don't think so. In fact, I'm glad they're avoiding us. Most of the time I'm too tired to receive them if they did want to visit.'

Then, when it was clear he would not recover, she noticed the wives melt away to another part of the supermarket, the husbands disappear down side-streets in the middle of the town.

'We are no longer useful. It is as simple as that.'

'It can't be that simple.'

'Not complicated, then, either. They work with sick people but they are not ill. They are outside and above all that. They have to be. They loom like gods in the eyes of most of these poor creatures. Now that I am sick I simply am no longer part of the necessary lie that works. I have to be shut out. Gods can never appear ill or wounded.'

'*You* never behaved that way.'

'I like to think I was a little different, but maybe not all that different either. Anyhow . . . '

The day before he died, he woke briefly, recognized her and said, 'I think we were a good pair,' and almost at once the heavy, monotonous breathing resumed. They were the last words he spoke, and broke her heart, but they were a deep source of solace in the days ahead. She lifted the cat from the foot of the bed, burying her face in the fur, and left the darkened room to the nurse who came behind her and closed the door softly.

'What do you think of all this?' Mrs Waldron said as she stroked the cat stretched like a lion on the dashboard of the car. The black cat suddenly yawned, rose to her feet and looked gravely down on the surging water of the Sound.

The cottage was by a stream beyond the village, well below the road, which gave some protection against the storms. At high tide the ocean covered the rocks on the other side of the raised road. When the tide was out, there was a long, bright strand between two curving headlands. The cottage was whitewashed in the traditional way, with a blue stone slate roof and a small porch in front. A garage had been added to the side that faced the stream, and a large living-room and bathroom were hidden at the back. Mrs Waldron loved the slow, crunching sound the car tyres made as they rolled down to the porch.

Each morning, before Eileen left for work in Castlebar, the two women rose and had breakfast together. 'I know there's no need for me to get up so early, but it helps give shape to the day.' After Eileen left, Mrs Waldron tidied the house, fed the cat in the shelter of the porch, watching her with an amusement that was pure affection as she performed her toilet, with ceremony and great gravity, in the black earth beneath the escalonias. Then Mrs Waldron read. Even during the busiest times of her young life in the town, if she had not managed to set at least an hour aside for reading she felt that the day had lacked concentration, had somehow been dissipated and lost.

Now her only interruptions were rare telephone calls—and when her reading brought her face to face with some affection or sharp memory. 'She had done more than she wanted to, less than she ought.' She found herself repeating the sentence long after she had closed the book, seeing elements of her own life and

people she knew reflected in it, elements of that life seen and
given a moral sweetness that was close to smiling.

'Smith told me he's given up reading!' her husband informed
her boisterously one evening years ago after he came home from
the hospital.

'What's so funny about that?'

'He told me it's too passive. He's going to concentrate on hill
and mountain climbing!'

'Then he'll be happier climbing.'

'Oh, love, don't be so serious.' He tried to waltz her away
from whatever she was preparing for dinner.

'Are you sure you've not been drinking?'

'Not a drop. But I intend to have a stiff drink before dinner.
We have to examine Smith's momentous decision. Will you join
me?'

Without reading, she would feel her whole life now to be
spiritually idle. All through their marriage she and her husband
had talked to one another about the good things that they'd
happened upon, that lightened and deepened life, gave recognition
and pleasure.

After a light lunch she rested and then set out on her walk.
In all but the worst weather she walked, and never varied it
unless the wind forced her in another direction, but these walks
were never as enjoyable as the ones she and her husband took
together in the last years when they were alone.

She went by the harbour. It was empty now of boats except
for four old curraghs resting upside down on concrete blocks,
roped down against the storms. There were a few wooden crayfish
creels along the short pier wall and these were also weighted
down, as was some torn and tangled netting. Passing the harbour
she could choose between several sheep paths through the heather,
but generally she went by the path closest to the ocean. The only
person she met on her walks that February was a fat little old
man in green oilskins with a pair of binoculars. Always he was in
the same place, resting in the shelter of a big boulder and looking
out to sea. Only after she'd passed him several times did he look
at her and nod. Then, sometimes, she was the first to smile and
nod. He seemed pleased, but still they did not speak. She thought

he might be a relict, like herself, who had taken up bird-watching, or someone just fascinated by the power and beauty of the ocean, ever changing. What did *he* see there?

A school fife-and-drum band marching past the cottage to early Mass woke both mother and daughter to St Patrick's Day. The weather was warmer. People suddenly seemed to be in better spirits. Along all the cottages on the road to the harbour, people were digging their kitchen gardens, spreading manure and seaweed, shovelling the rich, black earth. Some waved to her with their spades or shovels as she passed.

'God bless the work.'

'And you, too, Missus, when you're at it.'

At the harbour they were scraping and tarring the boats. A man was lovingly measuring a square of calico over weakened timbers before covering it with a boiling mixture of tar and pitch from a tin jug. She loved the smell of the boiling tar in the sea air. There was a crazy doctor by the name of Doorley she remembered from her childhood who believed in the healing properties of tar, and each summer he tarred his ten children from head to toe. All of them were disturbed in later life. One became a beggar on the roads. Two committed suicide. Though her father, who was also a medical doctor, and others complained about his behaviour, nobody was able or willing to bring it to a stop. Everybody was too afraid. Authority could not be questioned then, especially when vested in a priest or doctor. How rapidly all that had changed. Sometimes she could hardly believe it had all taken place in the brief space of a lifetime.

As soon as the weather turned, the man with binoculars discarded his green oilskins for a thick jersey of unwashed grey wool with a worn black suit and a cloth cap. One day she stopped to talk to him, and the stop became almost mandatory. He had worked all his life in England, near Didcot, on buildings and line maintenance. Tommy McHugh was his name. He had five children, all grown. When they were growing up he saw them at Christmas and a few weeks each summer. During the war he didn't see his family for four years. A child conceived during one visit was three years old when he next returned. Dog-tired after the boat and train journey, he woke in the morning to see a small boy standing at the foot of the bed, saying to all who'd listen, 'That's my Daddy!' His wife and he had never lived together until he returned for good. She thought it must have been hard for them to come together after such absences, but she noticed he never talked about his wife unless she reflected a part of his own life.

'Is it the colours you watch or the sea birds or just the ocean itself?'

'I'd not be stupid enough to be watching anything like that,' he replied slowly, a sly smile in his eyes. He looked at her with approval, as if she had laid a clever trap and he had danced clear. 'I'd have no taste for watching anything like that. I'd be watching those sheep over there.' He gestured towards the Head and handed her the binoculars. What were white specks beforehand grew into clear shapes.

'Sheep are very stupid animals,' he confided. 'Hardly a week goes by but one of them doesn't fall off.'

'What do you do then?'

'Sometimes you can get them back on their feet. More times they're finished.'

'Are you not too far off here?'

'You can see better from here than on the Head, and it's a cruel climb. The trouble is that it's a very tasty bit of land.'

From that day on he always handed her the binoculars to look at the sheep. Over and over he told her about his hard life in England, the monies he sent home out of every pay-packet, how difficult it was to pass the time after work, but fortunately there was everlasting overtime.

One day he had with him a beautiful black-and-white collie pup on a long line of binder twine, timid and anxious to please, its coat woolly still, and before long she found herself looking forward to seeing it each day. At first, the man was enamoured: he was going to train it into the best working dog on the island. But during the weeks that followed, as the pup grew into a young, eager dog, and the training proceeded, complaints replaced the early in-loveness and praise. Sometimes the collie was 'as stupid as the sheep' he rushed and scattered. She observed how self-absorbed the man was, how impatient. Increasingly, she disliked that the young dog was in his control. She found herself wondering what his wife was like and how had she coped with his return? Thinking of the man and his life, and the dog and sheep, without warning, a buried memory of her father scattered the day. It was summer. She was home from college. Her father was late returning from a round of sick calls. Lunch was already on the table, and she was standing with her mother in the open bay window, when her father's car came up the laurelled avenue and turned on the big square of gravel. Instead of coming straight into the house, he went around the car and took a whole side of lamb from the boot, placing a towel on his shoulder to carry it proudly in. The lamb was probably some payment in kind.

She saw no significance in the memory other than it had displaced this actual day of her life and the disturbance her observations of Tommy McHugh had caused. Her life with her father and mother had passed. Her life with her husband had now passed. Was her whole life, then, all nothing? Was it just what happened and the memory of those happenings, like the old classmate she had once chanced upon in the ship's restaurant during a Holyhead–Dublin crossing? The classmate had grown old, was only dimly recognizable, as she herself had grown old, having to be asked if, indeed, she was the girl at Earlsfort Terrace who played hockey and married one of the medical students. The memory of her father, though, had not grown old, had come to her out of all those dead years with more freshness and vividness than the actual sea thistle and heather between the rocks at her feet high above the pounding ocean. It could not all be nothing. 'A mind lively and at ease with itself is content to look at nothing,' she recalled a favourite passage from Jane Austen, 'and that nothing will always answer back;' and suddenly the recollection itself gave heart and belief to her walk. That was what always answered back, all that we had loved, all that we had cared for. Love is never tired or dispirited. Love is ever watchful and lively and at ease.

The black cat was waiting for her return to the cottage. She lifted her on to her shoulder and carried her into the house just as her husband used to do on his return from work. The cat, at least, seemed to have taken on a new lease of life since the move to Achill. She had started to hunt again and had brought mice and small birds, even a frog, into the bedroom through the partially open window as she had done in Castlebar when she was young. Other times she sat out on dry stones in the middle of the stream, gazing down studiously at the small trout streaking about or lying still in the pools. Mrs Waldron didn't like the offerings of the mice or small birds in the bedroom. She hadn't liked it in Castlebar, but her husband had said, 'What harm is it anyhow? It's her nature,' and as he had sanctioned it, she did not want to be the one to end it now. After meticulous crunching of small bones, she heard a vigorous licking, then loud purring as the cat curled into the eiderdown, declaring to all her own approval of the good, providing cat she knew herself to be.

In the evenings Mrs Waldron prepared dinner for herself and Eileen. Mostly they talked of Eileen's day, of practical things that concerned the house and gardens in Castlebar and of Michael Flynn. They never talked other than glancingly of the dead man, and when they did the conversation was quick to move.

Hotels and restaurants on the island began to reopen for Easter, and the Waldrons returned to Castlebar for two weeks of the holiday. Nearly all the family came back over Easter, but for no more than a day or two, and all of them arrived and left separately. After they left, Mrs Waldron was more eager than ever to get back to Achill. For the time being, Eileen still didn't mind the hour-long drive on and off the island. 'It fills a space where loss can't get in.'

The summer was unusual, dry and hot, with hardly any of the usual soft rain. The island became crowded. Motor bikes roared past. People carrying blaring transistors walked or cycled by the cottage. Wild music came through open windows of passing cars and into fields sloping down to the harbour where whole families were saving hay. There was much broken glass along the roads. Eileen had taken holidays and gone to France for two weeks. Then her sister and brother and their families came to the house in Castlebar, and there was much to-ing and fro-ing between the house and the island, so much so that Mrs Waldron was seldom alone. She was fond of all of them and glad to have them, but glad too to have two whole days to herself before Eileen came back.

The morning Eileen was due she felt too excited to concentrate on anything, and after feeding the black cat she cleaned the entire cottage. Then she went to buy some staples that were running low. Close to the shops she came on a van selling fresh fish and bought a sea trout for dinner. She thought it a lucky or happy omen for Eileen's return: though this place was surrounded by the ocean, it was difficult to obtain fresh fish. With all the preparations for the homecoming, she was later than usual setting out on her walk. Tommy McHugh kept her talking for a long time, and he was full of complaint about the young collie who cowered now more than ever when approached. This changed her mood so much that she took a different route back to the cottage to avoid them. There was a lack of feeling, of sensitivity, in the man that disturbed her, and she was beginning to regret ever having come to know him.

While Mrs Waldron was talking to Tommy McHugh, Murphy and Heslin came up the road to the cottage. They wore jeans and sneakers, and because of the heat they had taken off their shirts and knotted the sleeves around their throats so that the light cotton floated out behind them in the ocean breeze, leaving their torsos bare. Murphy carried a loud-playing transistor. Heslin had a large, canvas bag slung from his shoulder in which there was a pair of collapsible stools, swimming-trunks, three six-packs of lager and a deck of cards. They were both in their twenties, sold encyclopaedias for a living and had come to the island because they'd heard it attracted working-class girls from Scotland and Northern Ireland who were reputedly free with their favours. Heslin was the better-looking and more forceful of the two and was admired by Murphy. Three nights they had been on the island, and so far had had no luck with girls, even though they drank each night into the hopeful hours in several bars and discos. They never rose before midday.

The black cat was waiting between the gate and escalonias for Mrs Waldron, and when Murphy and Heslin paused she went towards them and rubbed her fur against the bars of the gate. As she had known nothing but kindness, she did not flee when Heslin stooped to lift her into the crook of his arm. She continued to purr as she was carried the first few yards from the house, but when she tried to get away he held her tight. Once she began to claw and cry he took her in his strong hands and thrust her into the canvas bag. The cat alternately tore and struggled, or cried plaintively, but every ploy she tried was ineffective.

They passed Gielty's Bar and the whitewashed cottage where Tommy McHugh lived with his wife beside another small stream at its entrance.

'You wouldn't be interested in a pint before heading for the bay?' Murphy suggested as they passed the bar.

'Not with the bloody cat.'

'What'll you do with it?'

'I'm not sure. We'll see.'

Cars passed them as they began to climb the Head. A gang of bikers roared past aggressively in red helmets and black leather, a blue insignia painted on the back of the jackets. Below them a solitary old woman was threading her way back through the sheep and rabbit paths. They kept their heads low as they climbed, but as soon as they reached the summit they could see the bright strand in the two arms of the bay, the high, dark cliffs rising on the far side. There were no boats on the ocean. They descended quickly, the cat crying and struggling in the bag. An ugly, flat-roofed concrete hut or storeroom stood on the road above the bay. The bikers had turned around, revving the engines before roaring back. There were a few cars parked in a lay-by past the concrete hut. A couple of families were picnicking on the rocks between the cars and the strand. The sand was as white and unspoiled as it had looked from the summit and was completely empty. The tide was about to turn, and they walked far out to the water's edge, a white froth marking the tideline, a gentle, dirty backwash of water and sand curling back underneath the froth. A single man followed them out and searched along the froth until he found a green plastic oil can which marked a set line. He then began to lift the hooks, freshly baiting each one with sand eels taken from a red plastic bucket. His catch was small, three little plaice, a dogfish, the white head of a sea trout. Before removing the head and rebaiting the hook, he paused in obvious disappointment: by the size of the head the trout must have been two or three pounds, a prize catch but for the seals. Murphy and Heslin were afraid he'd be attracted by the cries from the canvas bag, but he didn't appear to notice. Throwing a metal weight on the end of the line far out into the tide when he finished, he disappeared up the strand with his bucket and the few fish he'd caught.

As he disappeared, Heslin handed the canvas bag to Murphy. He took a ball of fishing-line from his jeans, made a running noose on the end of it and cut off five or six feet with a penknife. Then he found a long, flat piece of rock and knotted the cut end of the line round its centre. Gingerly he inserted his arm into the bag Murphy still held. The cat cried, then went still, and he searched about until he could grip the fur on the back of the neck. Quickly he slipped the noose over her head before she could claw herself free. The cat shot away but was held by the line and rock. More strain and she would strangle herself. She tried to claw the noose free but it was too tight.

The two men fixed the collapsible stools on the sand, opened beer bottles, placed a towel between the stools, and Murphy cut the pack of cards and dealt two hands face down on the towel. Heslin turned the transistor high and drank the first of the bottles of beer. Behind them the black cat struggled against the incoming tide. An oldish, wiry man with a white terrier came on to the strand and seemed to notice the struggling cat. As he approached, Murphy and Heslin turned their stools to face him directly, lifted their beer bottles and put the transistor up to its full volume. The man paused and then, very reluctantly, turned away. A few times he looked back before leaving the beach. By then the black cat, through drowning or struggling or pure terror, floated about like any lifeless thing on the end of the line. The tide now washed around the stools, and the two moved further in as they continued playing cards and drinking. As they did so, they looked back for a long time at the incoming tide, but they weren't able to pick out the cat being tossed about on any of the low waves.

Murphy and Heslin kept moving in, letting the tide take their empties. When the strand was half-filled, two curraghs were taken by a group of men from the concrete hut and carried upside down to the water. There were four men to each curragh. The men's heads and shoulders were covered by the black canvas so that the curragh looked like an enormous insect with eight legs advancing into the water. There they floated the boats and fixed the oars in their pins, and a white nylon net was passed between them before they rowed apart. After they'd stretched the net, a man in each boat waved what looked like a crudely made spear to a watcher on the high cliffs, who blew a shrill whistle by way of recognition. Heslin and Murphy stopped playing cards to watch.

The crude spears were made from the leaves of old car springs, sharpened to a blade and attached to the long poles. The men were fishing for basking sharks. The watcher, high on the cliff, was able to see the shadow on the bright sand as soon as the shark entered the bay, and through a series of whistles was able to tell the men in the boats where the shark was moving. Obeying the whistles, they rowed in a wide arc until they had encircled the shark with the pale net, and then they drew the net tight. They killed the shark with the homemade spears. What they had to be most careful of as they thrust the spear into the flesh was the shark's tail: a single flick would make matchwood of the boats. They could sit out there in the boats without anything happening for days on end, and then two or three sharks could come in during the course of a single evening.

Murphy and Heslin watched the boats for some time as they bobbed listlessly on the water, the men resting on their oars with occasional strokes to keep their position, but as nothing appeared to be happening they went back to playing cards. They kept moving in ahead of the tide, playing for small stakes, till they had the six-packs drunk. The tide was three-quarters full, but still the men rested on the oars in the boats out on the bay without anything happening. It was easier now to make out the watcher high on the cliff.

'I wonder what the fuck they're waiting about there in the boats for,' Murphy said.

'I don't know and I couldn't care less,' Heslin said fiercely as he slapped down a winning card.

The two men then decided to have a last game. Whoever lost would buy the drinks in Gielty's on the way back. Then they folded the stools and towel and put them into the canvas bag. Several cars passed them as they climbed the hill up to the main road. As there was an evening chill in the breeze, they put on and buttoned up their shirts. It was very dark in Gielty's after the sealight. They ordered pints of stout, and Heslin paid.

'Would you fancy a second?' Murphy offered as they rose to leave.

'No. We have the whole night to get through yet,' Heslin said. 'And if we hit fish we better be able to reel them in.'

They rose and left the bar and walked back down to the village. A white Mercedes stood in front of the cottage. Further up the small stream a boy was dabbling a worm in one of the larger pools.

'They must be rich,' Heslin said as they walked nonchalantly past the cottage.

'Wouldn't you just love to send them a video of what happened to the fukken cat?' Murphy replied.

Mrs Waldron missed the cat as soon as she came through the gate, so constant was her wait by the escalonias. She looked at the stone in the stream and saw the boy fishing, and then about the house, and thought no more about it. Perhaps she had caught a mouse or a bird and was sleeping somewhere. In the excitement of Eileen's return, the cat was forgotten. The presents she brought—a silk scarf, soft leather gloves and different kinds of mushrooms and herbs from a market in Rennes—had to be examined and admired. Readily, Eileen answered her mother's questions about the towns she'd stopped in, the hotels, the restaurants, the markets, the shops, châteaux, museums, cathedrals, but there was a slowness in the responses, as if something weighed on her mind. Seeing this, her mother concentrated on the preparations for dinner, content to wait. Over the sea trout, mushrooms and the bottle of dry white wine she'd brought back from Nantes, Eileen spoke about what had been on her mind since her return.

'I didn't like to tell you till I saw how it went . . . I was in France with someone I've been seeing for months.'

'I can hardly pretend to be surprised. Did it go well?'

'I think so. I'm afraid though that Father might not have approved of him.'

'What makes you say that?'

'He's not a professional man. In fact, he manages a supermarket. His name is John Quinn.'

'If he's decent and hard-working and kind, I don't think

your father would have minded what he was. I hope you'll be happy.'

'Did anything happen to Fats while I was away?' Eileen asked suddenly, missing the cat for the first time and anxious to change the subject. 'It's not like her to miss fish of this quality.'

'She was here all morning, but I missed her when I got back. I am worried but I didn't want to bring it up. She always waited for me by the gate.'

'Why don't we look for her while there's still light?'

They searched the road on both sides of the cottage. The ocean pounded relentlessly on the strand.

'She might come yet through the window during the night.'

'That would be happiness.'

Two days later, Mrs Waldron said, 'Fats won't come back now. Something has happened to her.' The sense of loss was palpable. It was as if the dull ache of the surgeon's death had been sharpened to a blade. He was gone, and now the whole irrelevant playful heart of that time had gone too. They counted back the years that the cat had been part of their lives. She had been with them almost thirteen.

'I sensed it at the time and now I know it. Fats marked thirteen years of intense happiness . . . years of amazing luck . . . and they could not last. Yet we had all that . . . It's hard to imagine now. All that.'

Eileen returned to her work in Castlebar. Several times Mrs Waldron set out to walk, but each time found herself without heart to go further than the small harbour. She was ashamed of her own grief, the continual sense of absence instead of presence, glancing down at the stream and seeing only the bare stones by the pools.

Then one morning she woke up determined to walk the whole way out along the cliffs. The previous evening Eileen told her that she wanted to invite John Quinn to lunch the following Sunday. She looked forward with an excitement that was as much apprehension as curiosity, and knew that most of the weekend would go into planning the lunch.

She read all morning, made a light lunch and set out. 'A mind lively and at ease can look out on nothing, and that nothing will always answer back.' Was her mind at ease? Love was ever watchful. But was there a final going out of the light, a turning of the face to the earth? The light would belong to others then. They would watch. They would walk in the light.

She climbed away from the harbour, at once meeting the stiff breeze from the ocean, and was so intent on her path that before she noticed him she was beside Tommy McHugh. His face glowed with pleasure, and he came forward with an outstretched hand.

'You're welcome back. I was beginning to be afraid something had happened to you. There's not many of our kind left now.'

'My daughter came back from France. And we've had many visitors,' she said almost by way of apology.

'You're welcome back anyhow.'

'Where's Shep today?' she asked after a pause.

'It got so bad he'd do nothing I'd tell him. He was driving those sheep mad. So I took him . . . I took him and threw him— and threw him over the cliff, and I have peace ever since.'

She heard and didn't hear. She could see the petrified black-and-white shape blur in the air as it was flung out over the water. She had to get away quickly.

'Well. I'm glad to see you too,' she said as she started to move away.

There was something about the abruptness of her leaving, her distracted air, that displeased Tommy McHugh. He followed her disappearing figure for a long time, then said in the sing-song, confiding voice he had often used with the young collie when the two of them were sitting alone together above the ocean: 'I don't believe any of that stuff about the daughter coming from France, or the visitors. I wouldn't entertain it for even one holy, eternal minute. Let me tell you something for nothing, lad. Let me tell it to you for now and forever and for world without end, Amen, deliver us, lad, that yon old bird is on her sweet effing way out,' he declared to the absent collie in a voice that sang out that they alone among all the creatures of the earth would never have to go that way.

GRANTA

SEAMUS DEANE
GHOST STORY

Katie had always told us bedtime stories when we were younger, with good and bad fairies, mothers whose children had been taken by the fairies but were always restored, haunted houses, men who escaped from danger and got back to their families, stolen gold, unhappy rich people and their lonely children, houses becoming safe and secure after overcoming threats from evicting landlords and police, saints burned alive who felt no pain, devils smooth and sophisticated who always wore fine clothes and talked in la-di-da accents. She had so many accents and so many voices that it hardly mattered to us if we got mixed up in the always labyrinthine plot. Now that we were growing up, all that had stopped. But she would still tell stories of a different kind, downstairs in the kitchen, if we got her in the mood and if my parents were not there. I always felt their presence was a kind of censorship on what Katie would say, especially now.

'There was this young woman called Brigid McLaughlin,' she told Eilis and me one afternoon, after we had helped her with a big laundering of clothes and were all sitting about the kitchen, Katie in the armchair with her back to the window and her feet up on a pile of cushions. My mother was asleep upstairs. 'Mind you, this was long before my time. I heard it from your great-uncle Constantine's mother, God be good to them both but better to him for he's in more need of it, the aul' heathen.' She laughed at that and fell to brooding for a while. We didn't stir. This was her way of telling a story. If you hurried her up, she cut it short, and it lost all its wonder.

Brigid had been hired by a private arrangement to look after two children, two orphans, a boy and a girl, who lived away down in the southern part of Donegal where they still spoke Irish, but an Irish that was so old that many other Irish speakers couldn't follow it. Brigid had been brought up there before coming up here to Derry, so the language was no problem to her. Anyway, the children's uncle was going away to foreign parts and he wanted someone to look after them and educate them a bit. Now one of the odd things about these children was their names. The boy was called Francis, and the girl was called Frances. Even

Photo: Martin Parr (Magnum)

in Irish you couldn't tell the names apart, except in writing. No one knows why their parents christened them so. The parents themselves, they had been carried off by the cholera during the Great Famine, though they were well enough off themselves and had never starved. Anyway, however it was, this young woman— Brigid—was sent down there to look after them. She had a year's contract, signed in her father's house. But she was not, for all of that year, to leave the children out of her charge and was never to take them away from the house itself. Everything she needed would be supplied, on the uncle's arrangement, by the shopkeepers in the village a couple of miles away. So off she went to this big farmhouse in the middle of nowhere to look after Frances, the girl, who was nine, and Francis, the boy, who was seven.

She wrote home to her father for the first few months, and all seemed to be well. But then the letters stopped. It was only after it was all over that people found out what had happened.

The children were beautiful, especially the girl. She was dark, the boy was fair. They spoke Irish only. Brigid taught them all she knew, every morning for two hours, every afternoon for one hour. But they had this habit, they told Brigid, that they had promised each other never to break. Every day they would go to the field behind the house, where their parents were buried, and put flowers on the grave and sit there for a long time. They always asked her to leave them alone to do this; she could watch them, they said, from an upstairs window. So Brigid did that. And all was well. But after some time had passed, and summer had waned, Brigid tried to discourage them more strongly, for it was often wet and beginning to get cold. Still, the children insisted. On one particularly bad day in the autumn, when the rain was coming down in sheets, and the wind was howling, she stopped them going. She wouldn't give in. And they, in turn, insisted. Finally, she put them in their rooms and told them that was the end of it. They could visit their parents' grave in decent weather, but she wasn't going to have them falling ill by doing so in such conditions, no more than their parents would want her to, or want them to insist on doing. After a big quarrel, the first they ever had, the children went to their rooms and, after a bit, when it was dark, Brigid went to bed. Now, would you believe this? It's the God's truth. The next morning, when she went to their rooms, what did she find? She found the boy was now dark-haired, as his sister had been, and the girl was fair-haired, as her brother had been. And they didn't seem to notice! They told her they had always been like that, that she was imagining things. You can imagine! Poor Brigid! She thought she was going out of her mind. She examined them all over, she questioned them, she threatened not to give them any meals until they told her the truth. But they just sat there and told her she was the one who had got everything wrong.

Right, says Brigid, we'll see who's imagining things. We'll go into the village. We'll go the priest. We'll go to anyone we meet and we'll put the question to them. The children agreed and off they went to the parochial house and found the priest in and waited in the drawing-room to meet him. Brigid sat down and then got up and sat down again while the children, polite and well-mannered as they usually were, sat before her on straight-backed chairs, quiet and as assured as any two grown-ups would have been. When the priest came in, Brigid went straight to him and said, 'Father, Father, for the love of God, look at these two children, Francis and Frances, and tell me what has happened, for I don't know if they're in the hands of the devil or what it could be.' And the priest, very surprised and shocked, looked at her, looked at them, caught her by the wrist and sat her down, shaking his head and asking her what did she mean, to take it slowly, tell him again. But the children, she cried at him, look at the children, they've changed, they've switched colours. Look! She pointed at them and there they were, looking at her and the priest, and they were the colour and complexion they had always been, the girl dark, and the boy fair. We told her, they said to the priest, we had always been like this, but she says we changed colour and she frightened us. Both of them began to cry, and Brigid began to wail, and the priest ran between them like a scalded cat for a while before he could calm things down.

Poor Brigid! She knew the priest thought she was going strange, and the children were so loud in their protests and so genuinely upset that she began to wonder herself. Especially as the children kept their complexions just as they had been for days and days after and during that time.

No matter what the weather, Brigid let them visit their parents' graves and watched them from the upstairs window and saw nothing wrong. But she couldn't sleep at night, for she knew, she knew, she knew that she had not been mistaken. She could clearly remember examining them—running her hands up the back of their hair, seeing the boy's skin that shade darker, the girl's skin the white and pink that had been the boy's. She knew she had not imagined this, and yet there it was! She lay in the bed clutching her rosary beads and telling her prayers and every so often shaking with a fit of the weeps, for she knew either she was mad, or there was something very strange in that house and very frightening about those children.

With all this sleeplessness she took to walking about her room and now and again she would pull back the curtain to look outside, over to the left, to the field where the grave lay. It was no more than a week after she had gone to the priest that she looked out one night and saw to her terror that there was a kind of greenish light swimming above the grave, and in that light she could see the children standing there, hand-in-hand, staring down at the ground from which the light seemed to be welling up. She was so terrified that when she tried to cry out, she could not; when she wanted to move, she was paralysed; when she wanted to cry, her eyes were dry-dead in her head. She didn't know how long she stood like that but eventually she moved and forced herself out the door and as she did she began to wail their names—Francis, Frances, Frances, Francis—over and over as she rushed along the corridor. With that, she heard them, in their bedrooms, crying out, and went in to find them wakened and terrified, still warm and dry, both of them, still with sleep in their eyes. She brought them to her room and put them in her bed, shook holy water over them, told them to pray, told them not to be frightened, made herself go to the window again and look, and all was dark—no greenish light, no figures of children at the grave.

The night passed somehow. The children slept. She lay in the bed alongside them and held them as close as she dared without wakening them. But when they woke and asked her for breakfast and what had happened, she went cold all over. For now their voices were changed. The boy had the girl's voice, and the girl had the boy's voice. She put her hands over her ears. She shut her eyes. Then she said she became calm for a moment. She knew she had to see. So she asked the children to come with her to the bathroom to wash before they ate. She helped them undress, even though they usually undressed themselves. And sure enough, their sexes had changed too. The boy was a girl, and the girl was a boy. And they paid no notice! They washed themselves and said nothing. She made them breakfast, she gave them lessons, she let them out to play under the apple trees in the front garden. She knew, she said, that if she brought them to the priest or the doctor, the same thing would happen; they would change back and leave her looking like a lunatic. She knew, too, that if she left the house—even if she could find a way of doing so, for there was little or no transport to be had and certainly none to take them as far north as Derry, and there was nowhere else she could think of—something terrible would happen. She knew now she was being challenged by evil, and the children were being stolen from her by whatever was in that grave out the back. Oh, she knew without knowing how she knew it. There was no question.

Katie paused for a long time. The clock on the mantelpiece ticked. Eilis was bending down in her chair, her fair hair falling over her face. I wanted to peep in the shaving mirror on the wall to make sure my hair was still dark. Katie went on brooding. A coal in the fire cracked, and little blue flames began to hiss. There was no sound from upstairs. Some families, Katie told us, are devil-haunted; it's a curse a family can never shake off. Maybe it's something terrible in the family history, some terrible deed that was done in the past, and it just spreads and it spreads down the generations like a shout down a tunnel that echoes and echoes and never really stops.

Now I wanted her to stop, but she went on. I wished my mother would come awake or that someone would come in and interrupt. But everyone seemed to have gone. In an hour, the house would be alive with people, Katie would rush to get the dinner ready, I would scrub down the deal table, Eilis would start clattering the knives and forks. My father would arrive, my mother would appear, people would be chattering about this and that, the radio would be turned on for the news.

A nyway, anyway, Katie continued, passing her hand over her broad, kind face in a circular, washing movement, there the poor girl was, locked in with something terrible, and the two strange children changing over from one to another before her very eyes. She wrote down in a notebook all the changes there were, changes from boy to girl, changes back to what they had been when she first came. Some of the changes were smaller than others. One day it would be the colour of their eyes. The girl's would be blue, although she was still dark-haired and olivy-skinned; the boy's would be brown. Another day it would be their height. The girl was a little taller, normally, but one day she was the boy's height, and he hers. One day, she swears, their teeth changed. She had his smile, he had hers. Another day, it was their ears. Another day, their hands. On and on, for thirty-two days she watched all these changes. The children continued to sleep in her room, and on seven of the nights throughout those thirty-two days she saw the greenish light on the grave and the figures of the children standing there, hand-in-hand, even while they were lying asleep in her bed in the room with her. By now, it was deep into November. She was living as if she would explode at any minute but she kept her panic down. When anyone came to visit—the priest, the doctor, a tradesman—the children were always as they should be. No matter how she watched, she never saw the moment of change from one condition to the next. Then, suddenly, everything got worse.

She was brushing Frances's hair in front of a long, free-standing mirror that you could adjust to whatever angle you liked. It had a wooden frame, a mix she said of two woods: one was called bird's-eye maple and the other rosewood. She wouldn't have known this, but the children told her. They knew every detail of every article of furniture, every piece of china, every item of cutlery, every floor-covering and wall-hanging, every picture and clock, in the house. They knew the names of the local people to whom the farmland had been rented out for pasture, they knew the conditions of the rental, they knew the grazing in the different fields—everything! She had just finished brushing the girl's hair and was giving it a final stroke or two when she looked and saw herself in the mirror, standing there with the brush in one hand and the other cupped in mid-air, as though holding something. But the girl wasn't there, wasn't in the mirror, although Brigid was touching her, holding the strands of the child's hair in her hand. She stood there, stock-still, wanting to fall to the ground, keeping herself upright by dint of her will. The boy was in the room at the time and he came over, asking her to hurry up and finish brushing for he wanted to go downstairs and play with his sister. He moved into the frame of the mirror and he too disappeared. Brigid asked them to look, and they did, and she asked them, could they see themselves? And they said yes, of course they could, and laughed, but uneasily. And they could see her too, they said. The grandfather clock in the bedroom corridor struck at that moment, ten strokes. She remembered that. She counted them. It was ten o'clock in the morning of 21 November. And that clock never moved a solitary inch thereafter. It stopped and it never started again.

Now she didn't know it at the time, but that was the very hour and day the parents of those children had died, five years before. They both died at the same time. And it was then that the children stopped going out to the grave every day. It was then they stopped the changes. It was then, she said, that she knew the two people in the grave outside had finally come into the house. She went to the priest and asked him to come and bless the house. He did. He walked all through it, bearing the host with him, saying the Latin prayers, throwing the dashes of holy water on all the doors, all the exits and entrances. When he had done, he asked Brigid why she had covered up all the mirrors in the house. She told him. He commanded her then to bring the children to him in front of the big mirror in the bedroom and he took off the velveteen cloth she had draped over it and stood them in front of him before it. And there they were, just as normal. He would have to do something about this, he said; he would write to the uncle and see what could be done. The doctor

would call and see her, and his housekeeper would come in now
and then to help her. At least January wasn't far off, and then
she could go back home, for the uncle would have returned by
then. So, all this was done. But when Brigid was left alone, as she
had to be, she felt the presence of the dead parents all over again;
the house was colder, and every so often she would see the
greenish light under the door of one of the rooms that had been
closed up, or fading away at the end of the upstairs corridor, or
thinning out to a mossy line in the frame of a window as she
entered a room.

Then one night, she said, they came for the children, who
were in her bed as usual. They lay there awake, unable to sleep,
and the little girl began to sing a song Brigid had never heard
before in a language that was not Irish or English, and the little
boy joined in. Brigid stood before them, a crucifix in her hand,
praying, praying, with the flesh prickling all over her. Those
children lay there, she said, their voices in unison, singing this
sad, slow air, and all the changes she had seen before passing
over them, one by one, faster and faster, until she didn't know
which was the boy, which the girl. The whole house was
booming, as with the sound of heavy feet on the wooden stair.
The greenish light came into the room in mid-air and spread all
over it, and with that came this whispering of voices, a man's and
a woman's, whispering, whispering, furious, almost as if they
were spitting in anger except that the voices were dry, whipped
up like swirlings of dust in a wind. The children stopped their
singing and sat up in the bed, their eyes standing in their heads,
their mouths open but without sound, their arms outstretched to
Brigid. She opened her arms to them, dropping the crucifix on
the bed, and she says she felt them, their hands and their arms,
felt her own hands touching their shoulders, and with that, the
greenish light disappeared, the whispering stopped and the
children were gone. All that was left was the warmth of the bed,
the dents in the pillows, the wind whistling outside.

She got the priest out of his bed in the middle of that night
and he came with her, hurrying down the road, buttoning his
long coat, telling her she should not have left the children, that
this was the last straw, she'd have to go home. But when they got

to the empty house and searched it and found no children, he began to accuse her of having made off with them and was going to get the doctor, who had a pony and trap, to go to the next town for the police. Oh Father, she said, do that. Do what you must. But before you do, come out the back with me. She led him to the grave, and there they saw, the both of them, the greenish light wavering over the mound of earth and, clear as a lark-song, heard the voices of the two children, coming from the heart of the light, singing, singing their strange song. The priest blessed himself and fell on his knees, as did Brigid with him, and they stayed there in the wind and the rain until morning when the greenish light faded and the voices with it.

The children were never seen again.

All the mirrors in the house had shattered, all the clocks stopped at the hour of ten, only the children's clothes were left to show that they had once been there. God knows what the uncle thought when he came back. Brigid was taken home, the uncle came to see her, she talked to him, she talked to everyone who would listen for maybe six months after her return, she went completely strange in the head and people used to bless themselves when she appeared and hurry away. Then Brigid stopped talking. Until the day she died she never spoke again, would never leave her room, would never have a mirror near her. Only every year, on 21 November, you could hear her up in her room, singing this song, in words none could understand, a song no one had ever heard, that must have been the song the children sang that night long ago, in south Donegal, only five years after the Famine. And the blight's on that family to this very day.

At last, my mother moved upstairs, the bells of the cathedral began to ring, and the noises of the world outside came dappling in as Katie blessed herself, laughed and shook her head at something, and told me to get the scrubbing brush and warm water for the table. Eilis sat there, her hair falling fair over her obscured face.

Notes on Contributors

Richard Rayner, born in Yorkshire, now lives in Los Angeles. His books include *Los Angeles Without a Map* and *The Elephant*. 'Rich Rich Rich' will be included in his memoir, *The Blue Suit*, that will be published by Picador next year. His account of the Los Angeles riots appeared in *Granta* 40. **Steve Pyke**'s collection of portraits of the world's leading philosophers was published last year. His photographs of World War One veterans appeared in *Granta* 45. **Ian Hamilton**'s books include biographies of Robert Lowell and J. D. Salinger, *Keepers of the Flame: Literary Estates and the Rise of Biography* and *Gazza Italia*, published by Granta Books. He is currently writing a study of Matthew Arnold. **Kevin Jackson** is associate arts editor of the *Independent*. He has compiled *The Oxford Book of Money*, due out in February. **James Buchan** is a journalist and a novelist. His book *A Psychology of Money* will be published in 1996. **Jonathan Raban**'s account of the floods in the Midwest in 1993, 'Mississippi Water', appeared in *Granta* 45. His books include *Old Glory*, *Hunting Mr Heartbreak*, *Soft City* and *Coasting*. He lives in Seattle. **Chang-rae Lee** was born in Seoul in 1965 and emigrated to the United States when he was three. His novel *Native Speaker* will be published by Riverhead/Putnam in the United States in March. **Helen Epstein** first went to Uganda in April 1993. She did not return empty handed: while she hasn't yet designed an Aids vaccine, she may have come upon the world's most effective cure for athlete's foot. Apart from scientific papers, 'Fat' is her first published worked. **Nuruddin Farah**, whose novel *Gifts* was published last year by Serif, is working on a book about Somali refugees in Europe. He lives in Kaduna, Nigeria. **David Kynaston** is working on a trilogy on the City of London between 1815 and 1986, part two of which will be published in May. **Will Hutton** is economics editor of the *Guardian*. His new book, *The State We're In*, an account of Britain's economic woes, is published by Jonathan Cape. **Larry Fink** teaches at Bard College, New York, and his work has appeared in the *New York Times Magazine*, *Time* and *Rolling Stone*. These photographs are part of an ongoing project on 'Power—its frustrations and abuses'. **Sam Toperoff** is a regular contributor to *Sports Illustrated*. His books include *Queen of Desire*, a fictional biography of Marilyn Monroe, and a biography of Sugar Ray Leonard. **John McGahern**'s novels include *The Leavetaking*, *The Pornographer* and *Amongst Women* (shortlisted for the 1990 Booker Prize). He lives in County Leitrim, Ireland. **Seamus Deane**, a poet and critic, teaches at the University of Notre Dame, Indiana. His first novel, *Reading in the Dark*, will be published by Granta Books in 1995.